E

Ryan Denton has given us ⌇⌇⌇⌇⌇⌇⌇⌇⌇⌇⌇⌇⌇⌇⌇⌇⌇
like eating frozen concentrated orange juice straight from the cylinder.
On the one hand, he shows the fatal error involved in our man-pleasing decisionistic shallowness and on the other the distressing vacuum
caused by our unfaithfulness to the plain call to preach the gospel to
every creature. Taste the tartness of the concentration in sentences such
as these: "The evangelism of the early church was not calculated to be
easy to accept. It was calculated to be impossible to accept apart from
the grace of God, which in turn gives him all the glory." Or sample
this and lament its truth: "The Christian church in the west has forgotten the attraction of scandal. In attempting to accommodate our
evangelism to the culture, we have lost the appeal of being a savor of
death to the dying." We should feel in our consciences the incongru-
ity set forth in an observation like, "We offer to build houses or have
carnivals for the lost, but we refuse to do anything that would cause a
gospel scandal." Ryan has given a sincere biblical admonition to us all,
both for theological seriousness and fidelity in our presentation and for
courage and obedience to the evangelistic mandate.

—**Dr. Tom J. Nettles,**
Senior Professor of Historical Theology,
The Southern Baptist Theological Seminary

I really, really loved this book. There is no dearth of writing on the
subject of evangelism but there certainly is a dearth of both the proper
practice and understanding of it. Pragmatism is the order of the day.
In a tragic misunderstanding of the parable of the soils, modern evangelicals believe they must make the seed more attractive or throw it in a
more winsome way to gain converts. The Gospel has been so distorted
and diluted as to rob it of its soul-saving and life-changing power. The
results have been tragic. Untold millions of people now profess to be
Christians simply because they have made intellectual assent to a few
basic biblical facts but have never truly repented of sin and surrendered
their lives to Christ.

In *Even If None*, Ryan Denton gives both a sobering assessment of modern evangelical methods as well as a motivating challenge for believers to do evangelism as God has prescribed it to be done. Far from hindering evangelism, a fierce fidelity to God's sovereignty in salvation gives us confidence that God will save His own when His truth is accurately proclaimed. It will also provide us courage not if, but *when* persecution against Christians increases. I have read this book once. I will definitely be reading it again.

—JUSTIN PETERS,
Justin Peters Ministry

Confusion and malpractice abound on the topic of evangelism. Much of what's out there is based on faulty theology, pragmatism, and the restless desire to fill our churches with more people. We violate the first principle of evangelism if we attempt to fill the kingdom of God and its churches by using unscriptural means and the wrong message. A sound understanding of how and why a soul is saved teaches us to be accurate in reaching out with the gospel.

In *Even if None*, Ryan Denton provides a comprehensive treatment on the doctrine and practice of evangelism in simple language. The strength of the book lies in its faithfulness to biblical doctrine, upon which our gospel presentation should always be based. The book will be useful in many settings: classes, one on one discipleship, Sunday School, homeschooling, and home bible studies. I enthusiastically recommend this book.

—PASTOR JOE JACOWITZ,
Christ Bible Church, Pleasanton, CA;
President of FirstLove Ministries

The title of Ryan Denton's book, *Even If None: Reclaiming Reformed Evangelism*, perfectly explicates the particular reasons why a non-Reformed approach to evangelism is disjointed and incongruent to the NT approach. Denton goes step-by-step in presenting the prescriptive NT method of evangelism, which highpoints the definitive work of God alone in salvation. Denton does a fantastic job vividly contrasting modern popular methods of evangelism, which includes a willy-nilly friendship technique, with the apostolic presuppositional method. Speaking from years of hands-on experience, Denton especially shows the tragedy of the unbiblical methodologies now regularly practiced in many evangelical ministries. Overall, the reader will be truly blessed by the biblical substance in establishing the proper method of gospelizing the lost as well as Christians.

—Dr. Edward Dalcour,
Faculty, Theology Northwest University;
President, Department of Christian Defense

Ryan Denton has weighed the evangelistic methods of the modern church and has found them wanting. Seeing the bleak situation, he calls the church back to the Bible and the biblical gospel. This excellent book is a strong corrective and encouragement for winning souls in a way that honors God and His truth. I pray that it is read worldwide and motivates each reader to be doing "the work of an evangelist."

—Pastor Rob Ventura,
Grace Community Baptist Church, North Providence, RI;
co-author of *A Portrait of Paul and Spiritual Warfare*

Even If None is written by a man who evangelizes on the streets, but remarkably, he doesn't rely on his personal experience to make its points. The authority of this book is Scripture. The wealth of Biblical references and exhaustive quotes from evangels of old are alone worth getting this book. Ryan methodically explains what evangelism is and what evangelism is not, and it's done in a way that not merely instructs, but encourages the evangelist who is doing it right, the evangelist who is doing it wrong, and the person not evangelizing at all. It's easy to endorse a book that rebukes those who evangelize in an unbiblical fashion, less so when you recognize yourself in that book—but I am thankful for it. I can't wait to get this book—and I've already read it.

—Sye Ten Bruggencate,
Absolute Apologetics,
Producer of *How To Answer the Fool*

This book is a carefully argued, thoroughly scriptural, and convicting assessment of the non-negotiable mandate of Christ to preach the gospel to every creature. I particularly appreciate the author's clarion call to preach the undiluted biblical gospel to our western culture, as well as his loving rebuke that in so doing, we must be message-oriented rather than result-oriented. How painfully this book confronts us with the neglect of Reformed Christianity to evangelize our Western culture with a gospel that is "unto the Jews a stumblingblock, and unto the Greeks foolishness" (1 Cor. 1:23)! May this book prompt us to repent of our sinful timidity, and stimulate us to be as bold as Paul who stated, "I am not ashamed of the gospel of Christ: for it is the power of God unto salvation to every one that believeth; to the Jew first, and also to the Greek" (Rom. 1:17).

—**BART ELSHOUT,** Pastor of the Heritage Reformed
Church of Hull, Iowa; Visiting Instructor of Missiology and Church
Polity at Puritan Reformed Theological Seminary; Translator of
Wilhelmus à Brakel's *The Christian's Reasonable Service*

I recently had the privilege of reading Ryan Denton's latest manuscript, *Even If None: Reclaiming Reformed Evangelism.* This is an excellent and much needed book. Denton makes clear both biblically and historically that rather than being surprised by opposition from the world, and sadly from the church, the preacher must expect strong opposition to preaching Christ crucified. Denton shows that the world has never embraced evangelistic preaching. Nothing, however, must intimidate him or move him away from proclaiming Christ to the lost. This book has stirred me up renewed in me the need to keep evangelizing, and to thank God for the privilege of proclaiming the excellencies of Him who called us out of darkness into His marvelous light. I pray that *Even If None: Reclaiming Reformed Evangelism* will do the same for you.

—**AL BAKER,**
PEF Evangelist; Retired PCA Pastor

When the term "evangelism" is spoken of in today's Christian circles, it is most likely connected with movie nights, skits, and bait and switch activities. Ryan Denton has just offended 98% of the Christian church in America by writing a book such as this. This book is a "drawn sword" aimed against the compromised and watered-down foolishness of most of the evangelism we see today. This sword must not be sheathed until every lie is severed and every myth destroyed, even if none will listen. We must keep our sword drawn until our King returns.

—**JEFF ROSE,**
JeremiahCry Ministries

I have to say Ryan Denton has produced one of the most important books of our day. I praise God for this book and stand fully behind it. Delightfully balanced and thoroughly biblical, *Even If None* is a real eye-opener. You simply MUST read this book! Give one to your pastor as well.

—**SACHA WALICORD,** Senior Pastor,
Grace Reformed Presbyterian Church, Orange City, Iowa;
Professor, Dordt University; Visiting Professor,
Akademie fuer Reformatorische Theologie
(Reformed Theological Seminary), Giessen, Germany

I am ashamed to endorse this book. I am grieved that I am a guilty part of the generation that so desperately requires this stinging rebuke, and urgent recalibration in our understanding, motivation, and methods of evangelism. May God use this book to help us to grow the biblical backbone to bring the life-giving gospel to our needy world, regardless of the personal price. O Lord increase our zeal for reaching the lost and use it for the salvation of sinners.

—**DAVID WOOLLIN,** Pastor,
Grace Immanuel Reformed Baptist Church,
Grand Rapids, Michigan

EVEN IF NONE

Reclaiming Biblical Evangelism

Even If None

Reclaiming Biblical Evangelism

Foreword by **CONRAD MBEWE**

RYAN DENTON

For additional copies of this book
or a Catalog write to:

FirstLove Publications
P.O. Box 2190
Dublin, CA 94568 USA

Christian literature on various subjects
can be downloaded free of charge at:
www.firstlovepublications.org.

Unless otherwise indicated, Scripture quotations are from the The ESV® Bible (The Holy Bible, English Standard Version®) copyright © 2001 by Crossway, a publishing ministry of Good News Publishers. Used by permission.

Published by FirstLove Publications, P.O. Box 2190, Dublin, CA 94568

ISBN: 978-1-7343285-0-9

Cover and Interior Design: AuthorSupport.com

Printed in the United States of America

First printing, 2019

And every day, in the temple and
from house to house, they did not cease teaching
and preaching that the Christ is Jesus.

Acts 5:42

Come fire and cross and the crowds of wild beasts.
Come cuttings, breakings, and wrenching of my bones.
Come hacking of limbs and shatterings of all my body.
Come dreadful torments of the devil—
only let it be mine to attain unto Jesus Christ.

—**IGNATIUS,** Bishop of Antioch, 108 AD

CONTENTS

FOREWORD

THERE ARE TWO AREAS of church life that we easily talk about in a very superficial manner but rarely engage in with any meaningful energy. It is the areas of prayer and evangelism. The church prayer meeting is by far the least attended and the church's evangelistic efforts rarely get any Christians to volunteer. Call Christians out for a social dinner and you will soon find that it is difficult to even have standing space remaining because the place will be packed. Then call the same Christians for a time of prayer or for some evangelistic activity and they disappear like snow under a heatwave. Any true pastor knows and bemoans this reality.

Since this is a book on evangelism I will skip our sin of omission in the realm of prayer and concentrate on the task of evangelism. Here is a book that should help us all to diagnose the malaise that the church suffers from today in the area of evangelism and to also enable us take drastic steps to address this malaise. I love the biblical integrity with which Ryan Denton addresses this matter. For instance, when he states that the modern craze for conversions as evidence of true evangelism has undermined the place of faithfulness, he has hit the nail on the head. Many individuals reading this will agree that this is often what has discouraged them from participating in what ought to be a real joy in life—sharing the good news of a full and free salvation from sin and hell through the finished work of Jesus Christ.

The author also appeals again and again to various church leaders who have a proven track record in the area of church history and evangelistic preaching. Men like John Owen, Jonathan Edwards, George Whitefield, Charles Haddon Spurgeon, and Martyn Lloyd-Jones are quoted frequently. Most of these authors are squarely within the Reformed tradition. They base their concern on a genuine desire to see biblical Christianity preserved in the church across history. It is from this concern that they criticize what was wrong in their day long before this generation saw the fruit of the lack of evangelism or of wrong evangelism that we are now seeing. We really need to hear these voices afresh today.

The greatest challenge we have is in understanding what evangelism truly is. We need to see that it is basically simply sharing the good news of salvation in Christ. Yes, we share it with the desire that those who listen to our message will respond to it in genuine repentance and faith. However, we must never confuse our desire to see fruit with the task of evangelism itself. Once we confuse the two, we will inevitably find ourselves skimping on the content (the message) and making much of how to ensure that we see more people responding positively to our efforts. This is what causes the chopping off of the mention of hell and the need to repent. It is this confusion that has continued to cost us a lot as a Christian church.

I love to use the analogy of catching fish (not very original, I know). The work of evangelism is like simply ensuring that the hook is firmly fixed in the upper jaw of the fish. I must leave the pulling of the fish out of the water to the Holy Spirit. When he decides to pull the fish out of the water, there is nothing the fish can do to resist the effectual drawing. As a person sharing the gospel, it is not my business to try to convert sinners out of rebellion and unbelief. That is the Holy Spirit's sovereign work. I desire to see him do so now that the hook is in the mouth of the fish but I cannot manipulate him to do so. My greatest joy is in ensuring that the information about the gospel is well hooked in the soul of the sinner.

Although we must not deliberately be obnoxious to the people we share the gospel with, it must be obvious from even a casual reading of the Scriptures that faithfulness to the gospel will result in some of our hearers getting enraged and attacking us. Like a lion with its prey in its mouth, fallen human beings will not give up sin that easily. They will attack the evangelist in order to quietly continue in sin. Sadly, some of the attacks will come from fellow Christians who have their sugar-coated versions of the gospel. The only way to avoid such attacks is to chisel off the rough corners of the gospel or simply stop preaching the gospel altogether. We must be prepared to suffer for the gospel. Those who repent and trust in Christ will be glad that we had the guts to brave the animosity of those who do not want to repent. Above all, God himself will be glorified in us when we are willing to jeopardize everything for the sake of obeying him. Even if none come to Christ, we should allow this thought to remain a great encouragement to us. We are doing what God wants us to do. The smile of his approbation is all that we should ultimately care for.

If there is one plea I must end with it is that a person who reads Ryan Denton's book should not simply read it for the purpose of increasing head knowledge but rather for the purpose of joining the growing number of God's children who take the work of evangelism seriously. We have done enough talking; let us fold our sleeves and get to work. We have the true gospel; let us ensure that it is communicated collectively and individually to those who need to hear it. Let us proceed to pray that the Lord will own our labors so that with the help of the Holy Spirit we may see more spiritual babies being born and nurtured in our churches.

Conrad Mbewe
December, 2019

PREFACE

THE PURPOSE OF THIS BOOK is to address the hardness of the soil upon which we cast the gospel in the post-Christian West, especially as it relates to evangelism. Several adequate books on evangelism have been written in the last half-century. This book is not an attempt to supplant them, but rather, to supplement what has already been said with the following applications.

First, now like never before our evangelism efforts in the West are actually generating outright persecution. Arrests, terminations from work, and doxing are already common experiences for many Western Christians. Eventually it could include martyrdom. This is not a doomsday scenario, but something already on the horizon. How do we respond to such a condition, especially as it pertains to evangelism? Should we be more pragmatic? Should we be less vocal? Should we retreat?

Second, how do we gauge our evangelism effectiveness, especially if it leads to hatred and societal ostracism? Western Christianity had a significant influence on the culture for several centuries. It is accustomed to "success" in some degree or another. Today it is no longer that way. When it comes to evangelism, what do we do in light of such circumstances? Are we still successful if our evangelism sees little or no conversions? By looking at Scripture and church history, these are the questions this book addresses.

Also, this book is not confined only to Western Christians. Unlike most Christians around the world, however, many in the West today are experiencing real persecution for the first time. Christians in other parts of the world and even throughout church history have always been treated as the scum of the earth. Western Christians, at last, are in the same situation. Now more than ever Christians must take ownership in the sphere of evangelism rather than allow ourselves to be influenced by synergistic approaches. Now more than ever we must trust in God's Word—not only for how to do evangelism, but to know what will happen to those who evangelize.

Lastly, the reader should not assume that such a bleak season in the realm of conversions and persecution means that this will always be the case until the end of time. On the contrary, the Scriptures teach that Christ has authority in heaven and on earth, and that He is King of kings and Lord of lords. A genuine outpouring of God's Spirit should be expected, even in lands that seem unusually hardened to the gospel. Whether or not we see it in our lifetime, we anticipate the day when such a scene will occur not only in the West but throughout the world. In the meantime, when the land is swarmed with gospel-plucking birds, what are our marching orders? When Jezebels and Herods roar at God's people, jailing them or worse, what should we do in regard to evangelism?

Some sections of the book have been developed from *A Certain Sound: A Primer on Open Air Preaching*, written by Scott Smith and myself (Grand Rapids, MI: Reformation Heritage Books, 2019). The permission to reprint these sections is acknowledged with appreciation. I would also like to thank my pastor, Joe Rosales, along with Jerry Minor and David Woollin who both read the book in its nascent stage and provided much needed suggestions. Thanks also to Joe Jacowitz who did the same after the book had been more developed. Most especially I would like to thank my wife, Tasha, who provides a habitual illustration of 1 Peter 3:4: "Let your adorning be the hidden person of the heart with the imperishable beauty of a gentle and quiet spirit, which in God's sight is very precious."

May the Lord use this feeble effort to advance His kingdom in the West and around the world, for the sake of His own glory.

PART ONE

RIGHT BELIEF

CHAPTER I

The Peril of "Even if One"

IT IS NO SECRET these are dry times for evangelism in the West. We look wistfully at the revivals under Whitefield and Edwards and wonder, "Was it really so?" We are skeptical when hearing of mass conversions taking place in exotic lands today. The motto in the West is, "even if one," which implies that the conversion of one person would make all our evangelism efforts worth it. But "the one" rarely happens. Day after day, we cast the gospel onto concrete soil. We see little interest in God in our culture and families. Biblical churches, in general, see little growth. Our song is, "The harvest is past, the summer is ended," and still none are saved (Jer. 8:20). Or again, "Who has believed what he has heard from us? And to whom has the arm of the LORD been revealed?" (Is. 53:1-2). The disciples asked, "Lord, are there just a few who are being saved?" (Luke 13:23). Without being facetious, we could ask the same thing.

It is also no secret that Western Christianity has been pulverized by watered-down approaches to evangelism, resulting in far more false converts than anything genuine. Carnality is now rampant in the churches in an attempt to please such counterfeits. The blame, in part, must be cast on unbiblical views of man and conversion. To assume man has the power to save himself based on a "decision" will also assume the preacher or evangelism "method" has power to coerce the person into such a decision. And when such a theology is faced with the barren season of our day, the preacher or method will inevitably manufacture some kind of positive "decision" from the hearers, even if doing so means compromising biblical doctrine. When spiritual drought is coupled with such a view of conversion, perilous and pragmatic evangelism tactics will flourish.

Most evangelism ministries today seem driven by a desire to not offend anyone for the purpose of "winning souls" in a numerical sense. The desire for converts at any cost has not only pestered the church but also demonstrates a lack of understanding regarding biblical evangelism. When someone thinks the primary motivation of evangelism is to "save souls," even if it is "the one," methodologies will spring up that guarantee such an effect, however spurious or unbiblical they are—and however sincere the users of such methodologies may be. When such a motive is brought into a society that is unusually hardened to the gospel, the natural alternative is to find ways to make the gospel and evangelism more pleasing to the lost, even if it means watering down the gospel for the sake of kindness and being inoffensive, thinking that this is the magical concoction for saving people.

The largest protestant denomination in the West provides an unfortunate example. When a potential church planter visits their North American missions' website, the first caption under the "Go" page is the following: "Every day of your life is an opportunity. God designed you with unique skills and experiences, and your story has the potential to reach someone in a way no one else's can. We want to help you connect your story to others."[1] Notice there is no mention of the gospel. There is no mention of Jesus Christ. Instead, evangelism and missions has become about spreading you and your story.

This is not an anomaly, either. This is the approach of most missions and evangelism ministries today, having their roots in Spurgeon's time, who said in 1888: "I confess I am deeply grieved at some of the inventions of modern mission work."[2] Jeremy Walker seems to be describing the last two centuries of evangelism in the West when he says, "So much of what passes for evangelism in our day is simply froth, aimed not through the mind to the heart and will, but simply at whipping up or playing on carnal emotions."[3]

Those who suffer most are churchgoers who unwittingly follow leaders advocating such approaches to evangelism. Because of the unusual hardness of the soil, churchgoers know their evangelism efforts are rarely going to see converts. They

---

[1] North American Mission Board (Southern Baptist Convention). Last accessed August 10, 2018. www.namb.net/go.

[2] Charles H. Spurgeon, *An All-Round Ministry* (Carlisle, PA: The Banner of Truth repr., 1965), 297.

[3] Jeremy Walker, *The Brokenhearted Evangelist* (Grand Rapids, MI: Reformation Heritage Books, 2012), 79.

know they are supposed to share the gospel, but they have been brought up in a culture, including at church, that emphasizes salvific "success" as the chief motive for evangelizing. And in an evangelism culture that puts the pressure of salvation on man's decision, and hence, on the person sharing the gospel to get man to make such a decision, they are ashamed of themselves whenever they fail to see converts. They feel it is their fault. They feel embarrassed when asked, "how many did you bring to the Lord?" Either that or they compromise the gospel to make it simple as possible to "decide" for Christ. Will Metzger describes such a feeling in *Tell the Truth*:

> I was motivated by an awesome sense of responsibility and increasing guilt because I was led to believe that I was unspiritual—or at least unfaithful—if I hadn't led someone to Christ.' So I uncritically grabbed onto various methods of witnessing.... Yet the criterion of success was a numbers game: counting those who prayed, raised a hand or filled out a card. I was a failure.[4]

One of the chief reasons biblical evangelism is avoided in our culture is the discouragement that comes from lack of results. Although it is healthy to assume God will convert the person we share the gospel with, it is unhealthy to assume evangelism is unsuccessful if God does not. And even though many readers would agree with this statement, we must recall the popularity of the phrase, "even if one," which clearly indicates evangelism has become defined by "the one" rather than by faithfulness.

---

[4] Will Metzger, *Tell the Truth* (Downers Grove, IL: InterVarsity, 1981), 15.

The same can be seen as early as the 1800s, when numbers and effects became the primary gauge for evaluating evangelism. Iain Murray documents that certain groups "made 'special-efforts' the hallmark of evangelism for the next hundred years and in so doing it inevitably induced discouragement over all that was not special. For in the special, supposedly, lay the only hope.... It never supposed that there could be no effective evangelism without revival."[5] The same is true of pastors who live in a culture where the number of baptisms or the size of the church is the ultimate standard of "effective" or successful pastoring. How many people come forward at the end of a sermon or how many people go to your Sunday morning service becomes the mark of "successful" pastoring, and so the temptation to preach "smooth things" becomes more prevalent (Is. 30:10).

But something is seriously wrong here. This kind of yoke was never meant to be worn by Christians or pastors. It is similar to the Pharisees and Sadducees yoking people with "traditions of men" (Mark 7:8) or the phenomenon found in Pentecostal churches when it comes to speaking in tongues. Anyone who does not speak in tongues in such churches is made to feel like a lesser Christian, if saved at all. And so what do people in such churches do? They fake it. Or, discouraged by their "lack" of spirituality, they leave the church. This was never the agenda of charismatic churches, but rather the logical outworking of what actually happens. When it comes to evangelism, most Christians either put forth some kind of truncated gospel

---

[5] Iain H. Murray, *Revival & Revivalism* (Carlisle, PA: The Banner of Truth, 1994), 384.

presentation or they become discouraged and stop sharing the gospel altogether:

> Evangelicals know that all is not well in their churches and missions. Behind the façade of glowing missionary reports and massive statistics there is a profound awareness that the church has little power in evangelism. While bravely trying to produce an aura of joy and victory among their followers, church leaders are uneasy and deeply dissatisfied with their present experience and the results of their efforts.[6]

This is further illustrated by the fact that many missions and church planting organizations in the West will pull support unless a certain quota of members or conversions is met after a specific period of time. It goes without saying this will influence the church planter to accommodate doctrine and church polity to those who would otherwise never go to church. This approach assumes that church growth and conversion is somehow directly related to the church planter. It assumes church growth and conversion is the work of man.

The Bible teaches that God gives the increase, not man (1 Cor. 3:6), and that salvation is of the Lord (Ps. 3:8), which is why the Scriptures nowhere imply that church leaders or Christians should set numerical goals for church growth. Noah, Isaiah, and even Paul would have been seen as "unsuccessful" by such standards, despite their unquestionable faithfulness and care for people's souls. The same is true of William Carey or Adoniram Judson, missionaries to India who both

---

[6] Walter J. Chantry, *Today's Gospel* (Carlisle, PA: The Banner of Truth, 1970), 9.

labored for almost a decade before seeing one convert. Will Metzger concurs, noting that "the question of whether or not we are evangelizing cannot be settled by counting the number of converts. In that case, many faithful missionaries who have seen no converts from years of labor would have to be rebuked for lack of witnessing."[7] It is bad enough the land is spiritually hardened. But now those called to evangelize in such an environment must either submit to the "success-driven" evangelicalism through manipulations and a watered-down gospel or give an account for why they are so "unsuccessful."

Meddling Evangelism

In a culture increasingly hardened to the thing of God, meddling with the biblical prescription for evangelism will always be a temptation. The pragmatic fire fanned by Finney and others in the 1800s has become an inferno in our day. The emergence of revivalism in America altered the view of conversion and ministerial motives, exemplified by Iain Murray's description of how the "altar call" came about: "Nobody, at first, claimed to regard it as a means of conversion. But very soon, and inevitably, answering the call to the altar came to be confused with being converted. People heard preachers plead for them to come forward with the same urgency with which they pleaded for them to repent and believe."[8]

C. H. Spurgeon himself gave "no public appeals at the Metropolitan Tabernacle...and he was against any regular use of

---

[7] Will Metzger, *Tell the Truth* (Downers Grove, IL: InterVarsity, 1981), 56.

[8] Iain H. Murray, *Revival & Revivalism* (Carlisle, PA: The Banner of Truth Trust, 1994), 186.

inquiry meetings,"[9] but he notes how such a change was felt on his side of the ocean by the end of the nineteenth century:

> I remember very well several young men who were of good moral character and religiously promising. Instead of searching their hearts and aiming at their real conversion, the pastor never gave them any time to think about their spiritual condition. Instead, he pestered until he persuaded them (not the Spirit) to make a profession.[10]

After Spurgeon's death in 1892, "things soon slid" towards pragmatism in his church, even though it was still Reformed in its theology.[11] Iain Murray summarizes, "If the apparatus for decisions is established, and the immediate public visibility of professed converts is encouraged, then the sheer weight of numbers 'responding' comes to be taken as indisputable proof."[12]

This is what we see today when it comes to evangelism. There is a frantic hurry "to get members into the church" or to have an "apparatus for decisions." There is a drive to preach "come forward" instead of "repent and believe." When evangelizing outside the church, there is a passion to see some kind of tangible fruit for the purpose of telling others that x-number of people accepted Jesus. Of course we desire to see people converted, but what is driving these desires to see, or perhaps better put, force results? Do we do it for "the one"? And if so, what if "the one" never comes? What if we never see salvific

---

[9] Murray, *Revival & Revivalism*, 410.

[10] Charles H. Spurgeon, *The Soul Winner* (Abbotsford, WI: Life Sentence Publishing, 2016), 4.

[11] Murray, *Revival & Revivalism*, 410.

[12] Murray, *Revival & Revivalism*, 411.

fruit? Do we accommodate the message? Do we present a gospel easier to accept or more "effective" in the realm of salvific numbers? Do we quit evangelizing?

The importance of answering these questions in a biblical way becomes all the more common in a society where, according to Jeremy Walker,

> We do not see the outcome of our evangelism producing, at the present time, a healthy crop of souls for Christ. We do not deny that a silent, private work may be still going on in the minds and hearts of some, but we may see no or few open professions of faith in Jesus Christ and few additions to the church of our Lord and Savior. Our gospel seed seems not to be falling on good ground.[13]

This is why we must probe our evangelism motives. Every Christian should aggressively inquire into the phrases he uses, especially in an area like evangelism. The phrases can be seen as a symptom of an underlying, oftentimes perfidious condition. The cause is usually theological or cultural. In this case it is both. A hardened state to the gospel, an obsession for "success," and a penchant towards pragmatic theology are perfect ingredients for such an unbiblical phrase as "even if one" to flourish. The phrase "even if one" shifts the focus from evangelizing for the glory of God and for the sake of obedience to the gospel to doing so for the sake of results, which belong only to God. Such a phrase implies that unless "the one" is saved, all our faithfulness has been wasted.

When it comes to numbering salvific fruit, Spurgeon

---

[13] Walker, *The Brokenhearted Evangelist*, 129.

exhorts, "Don't be in a hurry to count these supposed converts. Don't take them into the church too soon and don't be
too proud of their enthusiasm, if it isn't accompanied with
some degree of softening and tenderness to show that the Holy
Spirit has really been at work within them."[14] Again, "Don't
number your fish before they are broiled, nor count your converts before you have tested and tried them. This process may
make your work somewhat slow, but it will be sure."[15] Such an
approach makes it difficult to boast of swelling numbers when
reporting our evangelistic work to the church or inquirers, but
it is the only biblical way to evangelize.

Does A Harvest Matter?

The phrase "even if one" is like so many other catchwords or
clichés that take root in Christian culture but have little or zero
biblical basis. Like "The Sinner's Prayer" or "God hates the sin
but loves the sinner," the phrase "even if one" is nowhere found
in Scripture. But this does not mean we should not be concerned about "the one" in evangelism or ministry. The shep-
herd left the ninety-nine to go after the one, and as Christians
we should do the same (Luke 15:4). Heaven rejoices at the salvation of one soul, and we do as well (Luke 15:10). The salvation of souls is a warranted reason for evangelizing. Our duty
toward man is to love him as we want to be loved, and there
is nothing more loving than to share the gospel with him. We
want our fellow man, made in God's image, to know what it is
to have "fullness of joy" in Christ and to be reconciled to the

---

[14] Spurgeon, *The Soul Winner*, 28.
[15] Spurgeon, *The Soul Winner*, 30.

God of the universe. We do not want our neighbor to perish in hell, but to join us for eternity in praising the King of kings. By no means should we downplay the importance of evangelizing for the sake of men's souls. We desire people to be converted. Like Paul, our aim should be persuading others to be reconciled to God.

Rather, what is needed is a reevaluation of our primary motive for evangelism, otherwise we will deviate into man-centered territory, which is already the case. To assume "the one" is the chief motive of evangelism is evidence that a misunderstanding of biblical evangelism is afoot in the Western church today. What is needed is a return to the basics. What is evangelism? What is the goal of evangelism? How do we gauge evangelism success? The next chapter will explore these questions.

CHAPTER 2

Evangelism Described

MOST CHRISTIANS TODAY are likely to define evangelism as something that yields results in the sphere of salvation or church growth. These things are unlikely to occur without evangelism taking place, but there is tremendous danger here. Numerical yields of salvation and church growth should never be the aim of evangelism or ministry in general. Joel Osteen, Jehovah's Witnesses, and The Church of the Latter-Day Saints can grow a "church" numerically and get many "converts." But this is no sign of doing it biblically. Glorifying God through our faithfulness should be the aim, leaving salvation and church growth up to the Lord.

The New Testament rarely defines evangelism through the lens of results, but rather as conveying the gospel to unbelievers, which includes the call to repent and believe, as well as a clear articulation of what it means to "count the cost" of following Christ. This is why Morton H. Smith in *Reformed Evangelism* says evangelism is simply "to set forth the good news."[1] He makes the observation that "sometimes we think of evangelism as including the result...but evangelism should not be defined in terms of the results, rather, it should be defined in terms of the activity of setting forth the good news itself."[2] Again, this is not to say that conversions are unimportant. It is not to say that our motive for evangelizing is irrelevant. It is not to say that evangelism should be without urgency or passion. But it is to point out that evangelism is sharing the gospel with the lost, period.

J. I. Packer claims that the confusion about "present-day debates" regarding evangelism can be attributed to "our widespread and persistent habit of defining evangelism in terms, not of a message delivered, but of an effect produced in our hearers."[3] Some have pointed out that a biblical view of evangelism is one of the marks of a healthy church. This would imply that a church with a contrary view of evangelism would be unhealthy. So what is an example of an unbiblical view of evangelism? "One of the most common and dangerous mistakes is to confuse the results of evangelism with evangelism itself. This may be the most subtle of the misunderstandings. Evangelism must not be confused with the fruit of evangelism."[4]

For an example of evangelism seen through the lens of results, consider Darius Salter's comments in his book, *American*

---

[1] Morton H. Smith, *Reformed Evangelism* (Clinton, MS: Multi-Communication Ministries, 1975), 4.

[2] Smith, *Reformed Evangelism*, 4.

[3] J. I. Packer, *Evangelism and the Sovereignty of God* (Downers Grove, IL: InterVarsity Press, 1961), 41.

[4] Mark Dever, *Nine Marks of a Healthy Church* (Wheaton, IL: Crossway, 2000), 134.

Evangelism. He notes that Martin Luther defined evangelism as "nothing other than preaching, the speaking forth of God's grace and mercy, which the Lord Jesus Christ has earned and acquired through his death," and that Packer defines it as "just preaching the gospel, the evangel. It is the work of communication in which Christians make themselves the mouthpieces for God's message of mercy to sinners."[5] The above definitions are wonderfully biblical, as we will see, but Salter goes on to claim that "both Martin Luther's and J. I. Packer's definitions of evangelism are defective."[6] His reason is because "they leave no room for the evaluation of effectiveness."[7] By effectiveness, Salter means success in the area of conversions. It should not be a surprise, then, to find him later saying that "evangelism has failed if it does not result in the evangelized ultimately being seated at the marriage supper of the Lamb."[8]

Another example is "Church Growth" advocate Peter Wagner, who states that "evangelism has only been accomplished when disciples are made."[9] In another place, Wagner states that "preaching one thousand evangelistic sermons" and "baptizing thousands in water" is not evangelism unless "ongoing disciples of Jesus Christ" have been left. "I may have been engaged in evangelistic activities, but the people themselves are still unevangelized. They are not yet safely in the kingdom of God."[10]

Such statements are tragic as they are shocking. When it

---

[5] Darius Salter, *American Evangelism* (Grand Rapids, MI: Baker Book House, 1996), 22-23.

[6] Salter, *American Evangelism*, 23.

[7] Salter, *American Evangelism*, 23.

[8] Salter, *American Evangelism*, 29.

[9] C. Peter Wagner, *Church Growth and the Whole Gospel* (San Francisco: Harper & Row, 1981), 56.

[10] Wagner, *Church Growth and the Whole Gospel*, 55.

comes to conversion, the most difficult area of all Christianity to evaluate, we must leave such numbering to God, who alone "looks on the heart" (1 Sam. 16:7) and who alone grants faith to the unbeliever. Since the Lord is the author of Scripture, the Bible can use phrases such as, "and there were added that day about three thousand souls" and "the number of the men came to about five thousand."[11] But even here we see that nothing like an official count took place, since in both places the phrase "about" is used, which implies an estimation. This is much different than what is usually seen in modern Christianity today.

This is why posting numbers of "salvations" or baptisms was not a typical practice of our forefathers, including Spurgeon, Edwards, and Whitefield, all of whom saw large numeric success from their evangelism. They understood biblical conversion well enough to know it is hazardous to publish such statistics considering the spurious nature of "professions" in general. Spurgeon was especially opposed to the publication of "numbers" regarding professions and baptisms:

> What mean these dispatches from the battlefield? 'Last night 14 souls were under conviction, 15 were justified, and 8 received full sanctification.' I am weary of these public braggings, this counting of unhatched chickens, this exhibition of doubtful spoils. Lay aside such numberings of the people, such idle pretense of certifying in half a minute that which will need the testing of a lifetime.[12]

---

[11] Acts 2:41, Acts 4:4
[12] Iain H. Murray, *Revival & Revivalism* (Carlisle, PA: The Banner of Truth Trust, 1994), 408.

The Deceit of External Responses

This is not to say external signs are useless when it comes to evaluating whether or not a person is converted. In a sense they are all we have to go by. Rather, it is to say that external signs should not be the aim of evangelism. Communicating the gospel clearly and without compromise should be the aim, regardless of the results or external signs. Martyn Lloyd-Jones rightly claims that the supreme object of evangelism is to glorify God, not to save souls, and that the motivation for evangelism is a zeal for God, primarily, and a love for others, secondarily.[13]

Archibald Alexander wrote on the danger of external signs being used as a marker for evangelism in 1844, when Western evangelicalism was already engulfed by their artificial manner:

> The zealous preacher often concludes and laments that there is no impression on the minds of his hearers, when, if the covering of the human heart could be withdrawn, he would be astonished and confounded at the variety and depth of the feelings experienced. Those impressions which manifest themselves by a flow of tears are not the deepest, but often very superficial; while the most awful distresses of the soul are entirely concealed by a kind of hypocrisy which men early learn to practice, to hide their feelings of a religious kind from their fellow creatures. A man may be so much in despair as to be meditating suicide, when his nearest friends know nothing of it. The

---

[13] D. Martyn Lloyd-Jones, *The Presentation of the Gospel* (London: Inter-Varsity Fellowship, 1949), pp. 6-7.

attempt at immediate effect, and the expectation of it, is of the errors of the present times.[14]

The Bible also shows that evangelism will often result in a gospel call that is not efficacious, which is especially important to remember for Christians living in the West. This is presupposed when Christ says, "He that believes and is baptized shall be saved, but he that disbelieves shall be condemned" (Mark 16:15-16). The parable of the marriage feast in Matthew 22:2-14 concludes that "many are called, but few chosen." The Scriptures nowhere imply that, considering how often there is little to no success when evangelizing, we should try some other method or that it is not evangelism. Ernest C. Reisinger goes a step further when he points out that even damnation is a result of evangelism, and hence it is effective even when none are saved: "There are two results: (1) '...he that believeth and is baptized shall be saved.' (2) '...he that believeth not shall be damned.' Salvation is one result, and damnation is another result."[15] One paragraph later he states,

> When the biblical gospel is preached, there will be results, and God will be glorified...His justice, holiness, and righteousness will be glorified in the damnation of those who believe not. Many modern preachers do not like even to mention this aspect of the results, but it is clear in the Bible. When God reveals His mercy, He always reveals His judgment, and the Bible makes this very clear.

---

[14] Archibald Alexander, *Thoughts on Religious Experience*, (1844; reprint Carlisle, PA: The Banner of Truth Trust, 1967), 3.

[15] Ernest C. Reisinger, *Today's Evangelism* (Philipsburg, NJ: Craig Press, 1982), 11.

This means evangelism is always effective, regardless of how a person responds, since the Lord is glorified either way.

This is also why we can be truthful and bold about making sure the unsaved know the cost of following Christ, which was His own method of dealing with men's souls. Martyn Lloyd-Jones notes: "Go through the ministry of our Lord Himself and you cannot but get the impression that at times, far from pressing people to follow Him and decide for Him, He put great obstacles in their way. He said in effect: 'Do you realize what you are doing? Have you counted the cost?'"[16] Another writer points to the Rich Young Ruler as an example: "Concern for the nobleman's soul was not the supreme motive that moved Christ to witness to this sinner. Running even deeper within His breast was a love of God. Though induced by a desire to save men, Christ was primarily motivated by a longing to glorify His Father."[17] Because Christ's motive was the glory of God, not "the one," He was able to communicate the demands of the biblical gospel, however impossible they would be to accept.

Evangelism is Sharing, Not Showing (Alone)

The following are verbs used in the Acts of the Apostles to describe the work of evangelism: to testify (Acts 2:40), to proclaim (Acts 4:2), to preach the gospel (Acts 5:42), to herald (Acts 8:5), to teach (Acts 4:2), to argue (Acts 17:2), to dispute (Acts 9:29), to confound (Acts 9:22), to prove (Acts 17:3), to

---

[16] D. Martyn Lloyd-Jones, *Studies in the Sermon on the Mount* (Grand Rapids: W. B. Eerdman's, 1984), 207.

[17] Walter J. Chantry, *Today's Gospel* (Carlisle, PA: The Banner of Truth, 1970), 23.

confute powerfully (Acts 18:28), to persuade (Acts 17:4). [18]
On the contrary, phrases not used or implied in the Acts of
the Apostles to describe evangelism would include building
bridges, establishing common ground, "friendship evangelism,"
or entertaining the lost. Ironically, there is also no mention of
"love" in the Acts of the Apostles.[19]

Even biblical Christians can be influenced by unbiblical methods that neuter the offense of the cross. Even the
Reformed church has been influenced into thinking numbers
or "salvific fruit" is the main catalyst for evangelism. If we are
not seeing people saved or filling our churches, we have come
to believe we are "ineffective" and should try something else. If
someone is upset with us or calls us narrow-minded or bigoted
when evangelizing, we are tempted to go about evangelism
in a different, softer manner. This is not to say we should be
obnoxious or profane when evangelizing. On the contrary, we
should be respectful. Our genuine concern for the lost should
be evident to all men. We should exude love for our hearers.
But it is to say that our evangelism should not become man-
centered or pragmatic just because it does not see conversions.

Will Metzger describes the gospel as "a word message
announcing good news. The key Greek words connected to
gospel refer to communication by words, talk, speech."[20] He
also notes that "verbal communication (of the gospel) was the
means by which the gospel spread."[21] This is why anything that
makes the gospel secondary is unbiblical. "The key to bibli-

---

[18] John Stott, *Christian Mission in the Modern World* (Downers Grove, IL: InterVarsity Press, 2008), 60.
[19] Even though, of course, the chief motivation of evangelism was love for God and man.
[20] Will Metzger, *Tell the Truth* (Downers Grove, IL: InterVarsity, 1981), 32.
[21] Metzger, *Tell the Truth*, 32.

cal evangelism is not strategy or technique. It is not primarily about style, methodology, or programs and pragmatics. The first and preeminent concern in all our evangelistic efforts must be the gospel."[22]

This method of hearing the gospel is found throughout the Scriptures. Writing to the Romans, Paul says, "So then faith comes by hearing, and hearing by the word of God" (Rom. 10:17). When writing to the Thessalonians he says, "For this reason we also thank God without ceasing, because when you received the word of God which you heard from us, you welcomed it not as the word of men, but as it is in truth, the word of God, which also effectively works in you who believe" (1 Thes. 2:13). And again, when writing to the Galatians, Paul says, "Did you receive the Spirit by the works of the Law, or by hearing with faith" (Gal. 3:2)? To the Ephesians he says, "In Him you also trusted, after you heard the word of truth, the gospel of your salvation" (Eph. 1:13). This is where biblical evangelism comes in: "How then shall they call on Him in whom they have not believed? And how shall they believe in Him of whom they have not heard? And how shall they hear without a preacher?" (Rom. 10:14).

The *Belgic Confession* says something similar in Article XXIV: "We believe that this true faith, being wrought in man by the hearing of the Word of God and the operation of the Holy Ghost, doth regenerate and make him a new man, causing him to live a new life, and freeing him from the bondage of sin." Faith is wrought in man through the hearing of the gospel and the effectual application of it by the Holy Spirit. It is that

---

[22] John MacArthur and Jesse Johnson, "Rediscovering Biblical Evangelism," *Evangelism* (Nashville, TN: Thomas Nelson, 2011), viii-ix.

simple. Throughout church history, beginning in Adam's day, the Holy Spirit applying the proclamation of the Word of God is what converts the elect. The *Second London Baptist Confession* states that "the gospel is the only outward means of revealing Christ and saving grace, and it is abundantly sufficient for that purpose."[23] This sentence encapsulates everything that needs to be said regarding biblical evangelism, which is simply revealing Christ's "saving grace" to the lost. Such an approach is certain to be "abundantly sufficient," regardless of salvific results, which is the point that needs to be emphasized. Gordon H. Clark describes evangelism as simply "the exposition of the Scripture. God will do the regenerating."[24]

This is not to say evangelism can only be done through auditory proclamation as opposed to some form of written medium. Any time the content of the gospel is communicated to an unbeliever, whether through a gospel tract, the Bible, or something else, evangelism is happening. But it does mean words are necessary, unlike what we see in many ministries today, where showing the gospel is equated with sharing it:

> Some people might say, 'We don't have to say anything about the gospel. Our lifestyle will say it all.' Others might quote the words of that old song, 'They will know we are Christians by our love.' Still others quote the words often wrongly attributed to Francis of Assisi (1181/82-1226), 'Preach the gospel at all times—if necessary, use words.' But we ought to look carefully again at Acts 11 to see what the church did there. Believers spoke of the wonderful

---

[23] 2LBC 20:4

[24] Gordon H. Clark, *Today's Evangelism: Counterfeit or Genuine?* (Unicoi, TN: The Trinity Foundation, 1990), 274.

grace of God in Christ...They told people with words the good news about the Lord Jesus.[25]

Many Christians claim to believe what the Bible says about the power of the gospel to save, but when it comes to evangelism you will rarely see them living this out. Many will pray for people to be saved without ever sharing the gospel with the people they pray for. They will fly thousands of miles to build someone a house, trying to "share" the gospel by their deeds. They will spend months trying to establish a "relationship" with someone before sharing the demands of Christ. These approaches are not in themselves wrong, but what is typically left out is the communication of the gospel. Showing becomes equated with sharing, whereas in Scripture sharing has the priority, even though our deeds and lifestyle are consistent with the message. "Nothing hinders evangelism today more than the widespread loss of confidence in the truth, relevance and power of the gospel."[26] John Owen agrees, noting, "The way principally insisted on by the apostles was, by preaching the word itself unto them in the evidence and demonstration of the Spirit."[27] Even when derided or imprisoned by unbelievers, "Yet they desisted not from pursuing their work in the same way; whereunto God gave success."[28]

Biblical evangelism is getting the gospel to people. Any other "method" can be contributed to a lack of faith in the gospel and a disbelief in the sufficiency of the Bible, which

---

[25] Wes Bredenhof, *To Win Our Neighbors for Christ* (Grand Rapids, MI: Reformation Heritage Books, 2012), 48.

[26] Stott, *Christian Mission in the Modern World*, 63.

[27] John Owen, *The Work of the Spirit* (Carlisle, PA: The Banner of Truth Trust: 1967), 103.

[28] Owen, *The Work of the Spirit*, 103.

alone should be our guide for how to "do" evangelism. "Our evangelism must be based upon a dependence on the Lord. Our hope of results must be in Him, not in man's will or in any other faculty of our hearer. But it pleases God to raise dead sinners through the foolishness of Gospel preaching."[29]

God Converts, Not Man

The goal of evangelism is the glory of God, which is done every time we get the gospel to the lost. The goal of evangelism is not to save them, since salvation is of the Lord, not the preacher: "God never laid it upon thee to convert those he sends thee to. No, to publish the gospel is thy duty."[30]

This is why anything cute or silly or wise according to this world will only distract from the simple message of the cross. J. I. Packer deals with this problem effectively when he says: "If we regard our job, not simply to present Christ, but actually to produce converts...our approach to evangelism would become pragmatic and calculating. Techniques would become ends in themselves."[31] Plain gospel proclamation must be the goal of evangelism. This could include while at a church pizza party or some kind of building project, for example, so long as the gospel is being clearly communicated. It could also include a conversation at work, open air preaching, or a gospel tract left with a person at a restaurant. It would also include while at home with family. Packer notes, "The way to

---

[29] Chantry, *Today's Gospel*, 86.

[30] William Gurnall, *The Christian in Complete Armour* (1662; reprint London: Banner of Truth Trust, 1964), 574.

[31] J. I. Packer, *Evangelism and the Sovereignty of God* (Downers Grove, IL: InterVarsity Press, 1961), 122.

tell whether in fact you are evangelizing is not to ask whether conversions are known to have resulted from your witness. It is to ask whether you are faithfully making known the gospel message."[32] George W. Robertson agrees in his booklet, *What is Evangelism?*: "The Bible never hints that the herald is the converter. Persuasion or conversion is possible only when the Spirit removes 'a heart of stone' and replaces it with a 'heart of flesh' (Ezek. 36:26) and 'opens' it to receive the free offer of grace" (Acts 16:40).[33] Conversion is something that no human could ever do for another human. But what we are called to do is share the gospel, which the Lord shows to be the proper method for evangelism.

We must declare the gospel to all the world, including "that all people everywhere should repent" (Acts 17:30). We must wrestle with men's souls, pleading they be reconciled to God through Jesus Christ (1 Cor. 5:20). We must tell men to "choose this day whom you will serve" (Josh. 24:15), though the effectual call of the gospel is a work of God alone. God is sovereign in all things, especially salvation, even though He condescends to use "the foolishness of preaching to save them that believe" (1 Cor. 1:21). We must preach the cross and resurrection. We must preach repentance and faith in Christ, bidding sinners to come to Him, knowing that all the while salvation is a gift of God: "Can the Ethiopian change his skin or the leopard its spots? Then may you also do good who are accustomed to do evil" (Jer. 13:23).

Biblical evangelism is getting the Word of God to the people for the sake of God's glory, not "the one." This is not to say "the

[32] Packer, *Evangelism and the Sovereignty of God*, 41.
[33] George W. Robertson, *What is Evangelism?* (Phillipsburg, NJ: P&R, 2013), 6.

one" does not matter. It is not to say that people are irrelevant when it comes to evangelism. On the contrary, our love for our neighbor should also be a catalyst, especially when it comes to our tone, approach, and urgency. But our primary aim is God's glory, which abounds all the more any time we speak of Christ. Whether at work, a college campus, downtown, at an abortion clinic, on the phone with a relative, at home with our family, get the gospel to the lost. What happens next is up to God. John MacArthur writes, "Evangelism is a privileged calling. We do what we can to spread the gospel wherever we are able. Then we go home and go to sleep. If we have worked hard we can sleep well, knowing, as the farmer did, that the growth does not depend on us."[34]

---

[34] John MacArthur, "Theology of Sleep," *Evangelism* (Nashville, TN: Thomas Nelson, 2011), 17.

CHAPTER 3

The Hope of
Reformed Evangelism

THE VIEW THAT THE SALVATION OF SOULS is not the chief end of evangelism has been criticized by many evangelicals. Like "Church Growth" pundit Donald A. McGavran, such critics argue that "going everywhere and preaching the gospel" is not evangelism.[1] To be fair, evangelism should be concerned with discipleship and its connection to local churches. But such concerns and connections do not qualify it as evangelism. McGavron disagrees, claiming that such a view is simply a way to justify the lack of salvific success: "Christian missions needed a theology that would undergird it during the long

---

[1] Donald A. McGavron, *Understanding Church Growth* (Grand Rapids, MI: Wm. B. Eerdmans, 1970), 24.

years when it was weak at home and hard beset abroad."[2] He says in another place that because of small growth in church membership, such a view of evangelism is a way "to find a rationale for existence and continuance that did not depend on numbers of converts."[3]

McGavran is not alone in his assumption, although the division is usually made along theological lines. Arminians take the approach that conversion is in part a product of man's cooperation or choice, and thus salvific results are necessary if it is to be called evangelism. We should be able to achieve such salvific results through mere persuasion and persistence. Reformed Christians believe salvation is a product of God alone, even though He uses means to accomplish this purpose. Salvation is not something that can be scientifically manipulated since God alone grants faith.

Modern evangelism assumes everyone but God should have a choice in matters of their salvation. On the contrary, the Bible shows that God has the right to save some and not others, according to His will. The desperate need for evangelism in the post-Christian West is undeniable, but only to the extent that it is done in a biblical and God-honoring way, which only Reformed theology can provide. The Puritan Stephen Charnock had no difficulty attributing salvation to God alone, seeing that its basis comes directly from Scripture:

> What is the reason he engrafts one man into the true Vine, and lets the other remain a wild olive?.... Why doth he strike off the chains from some, and tear the veil from the

---

[2] McGavron, *Understanding Church Growth*, 24.
[3] McGavron, *Understanding Church Growth*, 26.

heart, while he leaves others under their natural slavery and Egyptian darkness? Why do some lie under the bands of death, while another is raised to a spiritual life? What reason is there for all this but his absolute will?[4]

Someone who believes God saves irrespective of a person's "cooperation" or "choice" will go about evangelism much differently than someone who holds that God and man have a mutual part in salvation. This is why theology is so critical when it comes to communicating the gospel. The Bible is unapologetically monergistic, which means "salvation is of the Lord" (Psalm 3:8; Jonah 2:9) and is the result of divine election from before the foundation of the world, without any foreseen merit in the one elected. Apart from God's saving grace, founded on His unconditional election, men will never "choose" to follow Christ, regardless of how eloquently we preach or how attractive our gimmicks. Jesus told us "a man can receive nothing unless it has been given to him from heaven" (John 3:27), which includes faith. God's grace is the only hope man has to be saved, and consequently, regarding evangelism, the only hope we have when sharing the gospel. God must "rend the heavens and come down" (Is. 64:1).

God's unconditional election should be a great comfort to the Christian since it is not up to him to save sinners. The Christian does not need to rely on props or tricks when it comes to evangelism, since "no one can come to Me unless the Father who sent Me draws him" (John 6:44). Will Metzger shows this in *Tell the Truth*: "A clear understanding that

---

[4] Stephen Charnock, *The Existence and Attributes of God*, (1853; reprint Grand Rapids, MI: Baker Books, 2005), 398.

success in evangelism is a result of God's initiating grace frees the evangelist from false guilt when conversions have not happened. This does not necessarily mean evangelism is not being done."[5]

This is why the Christian does not need to use "shock and awe" or "bait and switch" tactics. He does not need to hand out ritzy gospel tracts in order to trick someone into taking them. He does not need to wait until a friendship has been established, fearing that otherwise the gospel will offend the person and push him away from Christ. The only instruments he needs are intercessory prayer and the gospel.

This was the view not only of the Apostles, but the Reformers and Puritans as well. Louis Berkhof notes that "according to Calvin the gospel call is not in itself effective but is made efficacious by the operation of the Holy Spirit, when He savingly applies the Word to the heart of man; and it is so applied only in the hearts and lives of the elect. Thus, the salvation of man remains the work of God from the very beginning."[6] Speaking about the gospel, Stephen Charnock notes:

> It has sometimes conquered its thousands (Acts, ii.41); at another time scarce its tens; sometimes the harvest has been great, when the laborers have been but few; at another time it has been small, when the laborers have been many; sometimes whole sheaves; at another time scarce gleanings. The evangelical net has been sometimes full at a cast, and at every cast; at another time many have labored all night, and day too, and catched nothing....

[5] Will Metzger, *Tell the Truth* (Downers Grove, IL: InterVarsity, 1981),163.

[6] Louis Berkhof, *Systematic Theology* (Carlisle, PA: The Banner of Truth, 1958), 459.

The gospel chariot doth not always return with captives chained to the sides of it, but sometimes blurred and reproached, wearing the marks of hell's spite, instead of imprinting the marks of its own beauty. In Corinth it triumphed over many people (Acts, xviii.10); in Athens it is mocked, and gathers but a few clusters (Acts, xvii.32,34).[7]

Since God is sovereign in salvation and man incapable of being "born again" apart from God's regenerating grace, the Christian can go out in total dependence on God. He will be liberated from the burden of "saying the right thing" or the fear he will say "the wrong thing." He cannot push people "further" away from God. People whose minds are set on the flesh are "hostile to God" (Rom. 8:7) and can't be "pushed" any further than they already are. Since evangelism is not about producing converts but rather being faithful in delivering the gospel, the mark of "successful" evangelism cannot be interpreted by how many persons are saved. This allows the Christian to focus on sharing the content of the gospel, not his own devices. Even if the "gospel chariot" returns "blurred and reproached, wearing the marks of hell's spite," the laborer can rejoice, knowing that only God can replace "a heart of stone" with "a heart of flesh" (Ez. 36:26), but he himself has been faithful to proclaim the gospel.

This is not to say we are satisfied if no one is saved, but rather that God is glorified through the proclamation of the gospel, regardless of the results. John MacArthur points out the great advantage of God's sovereignty when evangelizing: "We know when we witness or preach that God has His chosen

---

ones who will respond positively, and that should encourage us to be faithful. Election is not an excuse for inactivity. Those who think they can remain idle and leave it to God to save the elect through some mystical means do not understand the Scriptures."[8]

Belief in God's unconditional election should also keep the Christian humble when evangelizing. It will never be his "cleverness of speech or worldly wisdom" (1 Cor. 1:17) that saves or attracts sinners to Jesus Christ. The Christian must avoid assuming he has anything to do with someone's salvation, apart from sharing the gospel with them. The work is too important. The lost are too dead. This should motivate the Christian to be constant in prayer and to be a vessel set apart as holy, "fit for the master's use" (2 Tim. 2:21). The Christian must remember he is preaching to dry bones and that "the wicked in his proud countenance does not seek God; God is in none of his thoughts" (Ps. 10:4). Without this understanding the Christian will try to entice the person's emotions in unbiblical ways. He will attempt to speak cleverly or trick an unbeliever in order to "draw" him to Christ, which is exactly opposite of Paul, who was "unskilled as a speaker" (2 Cor. 11:6).

Any fruit or salvific success from evangelism cannot be attributed to the Christian, since salvation *is not of him who wills,* nor of him who runs, but of God who shows mercy" (Rom. 9:16). If the Christian sees bones rattle to life, he will know he was sharing the gospel with a dead man. He will know it is no credit of his that someone was raised to "newness of life" (Rom. 6:4). He will glorify God, not his own ability, since

---

[8] John MacArthur, *Ashamed of the Gospel* (Wheaton, IL: Crossway Books, 1993), 180.

it was God who was "ready to be sought by those who did not ask for Me; I was ready to be found by those who did not seek Me" (Isa. 65:1).

This does not mean the Christian should not study to show himself "approved" (2 Tim. 2:15). It does not mean the Christian should be sloppy or uncouth in his delivery of the gospel. It does not mean the Christian should leave off pleading with the lost to turn to Christ. It does not mean that Christian should not live in a way that is consistent with the gospel he proclaims. It means the Christian will be prevented of two mindsets, both equally harmful. The first one is discouragement. Packer points out that many Christians would quit evangelizing if not for the sovereignty of God in salvation:

> Faith in the sovereignty of God's government and grace is the only thing that can sustain it, for it is the only thing that give us the resilience that we need if we are to evangelize boldly and persistently, and not be daunted by temporary setbacks. So far from being weakened by this faith, therefore, evangelism will inevitably be weak and lack staying power without it.[9]

If there is ever a ministry where "staying power" is needed, it is in the sphere of evangelism, especially in our day. From the perspective of "things seen" it can be some of the most unrewarding work there is. Knowing God is sovereign will often be the only comfort the Christian has. William Carey provides a remarkable example of this during the early days of ministry in India: "I am very fruitless and almost useless but the Word and

---

[9] Packer, *Evangelism and the Sovereignty of God*, 10.

the attributes of God are my hope, and my confidence, and my joy, and I trust that his glorious designs will undoubtedly be answered."[10] Iain Murray remarks of Carey, "The obstacles were immense. Problems of poverty and illness, overshadowed by the darker burden of a land where in Carey's words, 'ten thousand ministers would find scope for their powers,' were constantly with them. Through the first five and a half years they saw not a single Indian convert."[11] Carey would go on to see revival several years later, but when times were difficult, it was God's sovereignty that buoyed him along.

Monergism or Synergism—Why It Matters[12]

A synergistic position takes away from the glory of God and leads to pride and false conversions. A synergist is always obligated to do all he can to manipulate the will of man into "choosing" God. This kind of evangelism will attempt to attract men with ritzy methods or eloquent and soft-peddled attractions, not the gospel. The notion of libertarian free will as it pertains to salvation is essentially in the same family as the Roman Catholic works-based system. It claims Christ has done His part, now you must do yours. Christ did a little, now you do a little. But if a person has to choose Christ in order to be saved, what does choosing entail? Walking an aisle? Saying a prayer? Raising a hand? Getting baptized? Anything the synergist puts forward will by default make it

---

[10] William Carey to Mary Carey and Ann Hobson, December 22, 1796, in *The Journal and Selected Letters of William Carey*, ed. Terry G. Carter (Macon, GA: Smyth & Helwys, 2000), 249.

[11] Iain H. Murray, *The Puritan Hope* (Carlisle, PA: The Banner of Truth, 1971), 140.

[12] This section has been developed from *A Certain Sound: A Primer on Open Air Preaching*, written by Scott Smith and myself (Grand Rapids, MI: Reformation Heritage Books, 2019).

works-based. "The very reason many contemporary churches embrace pragmatic methodology is that they lack any understanding of God's sovereignty in the salvation of the elect. They lose confidence in the power of the preached gospel to reach hardened unbelievers. That's why they approach evangelism as a marketing problem."[13]

The Bible shows man is saved because God gives them a new heart (Ezek. 36:26), and in doing so, man repents and believes the gospel. God raises the spiritually dead to life. God loosens the shackles of sin. The only choice when it comes to salvation is God's, and rightly so. Christ prayed, "Thy will be done" (Matt. 6:10), not man's, because man's will is undone. The monergist gives all the glory to God because salvation is all of the Lord:

> I am concerned that if you don't believe...that the gospel is the good news of God's action, the Father electing, the Son dying, the Spirit drawing; and conversion is only our response to God's giving us the grace-gifts of repentance and faith; and that evangelism is our simple, faithful, prayerful telling of this good news—then you will actually damage the evangelistic mission of the church by making false converts and filling churches with people who don't really know Jesus.[14]

Do Reformed Christians Evangelize? What's the Point?

Some think that belief in the doctrine of God's unconditional election will produce a lack of zeal in evangelism, but history

---

[13] MacArthur, *Ashamed of the Gospel*, 167.
[14] Mark Dever, *Nine Marks of a Healthy Church* (Wheaton, IL: Crossway, 2000), 151.

shows the opposite: "This doctrine does not hinder the work of mission, but powerfully energizes it. Through the preaching of men the elect will be gathered in. Therefore, the gospel must be preached by men!"[15] Wes Bredenhof observes that "even when the mission work of the church does not appear successful from a human perspective, God's purposes will never be frustrated. Whether through one missionary or another, whether through one sermon or another, through whatever means He chooses, God will gather His elect."[16]

This is why Stephen Lawson can show that the history of evangelism is filled with men who believed in the doctrines of grace:

> Far from paralyzing these spiritual giants, the doctrines of grace kindled within their hearts a reverential awe for God that humbled their souls before His throne. The truths of divine sovereignty emboldened these men to rise up and advance the cause of Christ on earth...The doctrines of grace ignited them to serve God in their divinely appointed hour of history, leaving a godly inheritance for future generations.[17]

Speaking about William Carey, Lawson says "he also put the lie to the notion that Calvinism and missions don't mix. Far from holding to a view of God's sovereignty that sees no place for missions and evangelism, Carey was consumed with passion

---

[15] Wes Bredenhof, *To Win Our Neighbors for Christ* (Grand Rapids, MI: Reformation Heritage Books, 2012), 82.

[16] Bredenhof, *To Win Our Neighbors for Christ*, 83.

[17] Stephen J. Lawson, "Introduction" to *The Missionary Fellowship of William Carey* (Sanford, FL: Reformation Trust Publishing, 2018), xii.

for God's power to convert sinners as revealed in the gospel."[18] Andrew Fuller, the Reformed preacher who Spurgeon considered the "greatest theologian" of the nineteenth century, not only gave hearty approval of world evangelism, but contended it could only be done through "God's time-honored method of planting churches and winning the lost."[19] Contrary to popular caricatures, John Calvin himself was zealous about evangelism and did more for the promotion of the gospel than most of his critics:

> Calvin made Geneva the base camp for an intensive evangelistic effort in France. Between 1555 and 1562 Calvin and his colleagues sent eighty-eight evangelists to France. God blessed their efforts because by 1559 the Huguenots (French Calvinists) numbered over one hundred thousand. In 1555 Calvin commissioned a missionary to go to Brazil. All of this reflected Calvin's understanding of the Great Commission.[20]

Another writer notes that "the greatest evangelists in the history of the Christian church have believed that salvation is by God's election." He then goes on to name Whitefield, Edwards, Carey, Judson, Spurgeon, D. Martyn Lloyd-Jones, and Francis Schaeffer as examples.[21]

---

[18] Lawson, "Introduction" to *The Missionary Fellowship of William Carey*, xiii.

[19] Michael H.G. Haykin, *The Missionary Fellowship of William Carey* (Sanford, FL: Reformation Trust Publishing, 2018), 57.

[20] John Mark Terry, *Evangelism: A Concise History* (New York, NY: Broadman & Holman, 1994), 79.

[21] Mark Dever, *Nine Marks of a Healthy Church*, 151.

The Procrastinating Spirit

Reformed evangelism is the only God-glorifying, God-reliant approach that exists. The Reformed Christian, when consistent, has the greatest hope and motivation when it comes to evangelism. And yet, if we are honest, we have to admit that the Reformed church is woefully behind other groups when it comes to evangelism. Reformed believers have no problem criticizing the Mormons or Jehovah's Witnesses in matters of theology, and rightly so, but these are also the groups proselytizing up and down our streets. We look down upon Arminian theology, and rightly so, but when it comes to evangelism, who would deny that their energy often exposes our sluggishness? We are quick to judge how wrong the cults and Arminians and even some zealous Calvinists evangelize, but we are typically tardy when it comes to evangelizing ourselves. We love our studies and our books and our exegesis and our conferences, and rightly so, but do they come at the expense of the lost? Spurgeon seems to be speaking of many contemporary Reformed believers when he says:

> On Sunday these loafers must be well fed. They look out for such sermons as will feed their souls. The thought does not occur to these people that there is something else to be done besides feeding. Soul-saving is pushed into the background! The crowds are perishing at their gates! The multitudes with their sins defile the air! The age is getting worse and worse and man, by a process of evolution, is evolving into a devil! And yet these people want pleasant things preached to them! They eat the fat, drink the sweet and they crowd to the feast of fat things, full of marrow

and wines on the less, well refined spiritual festivals are their delight! Sermons, conferences, Bible reading, and so forth, are sought after, but regular service in other ways is neglected. Not a hand's turn will they do! They gird on no armor, they grasp no sword, they wield no sling, they throw no stone. No, they have gotten their possession, they know they have, and they sit down in carnal security, satisfied to do nothing![22]

Reformed Christians are theologically sound, our churches are orderly and regulative, but a certain sleepiness seems to haunt us when it comes to the lost. We seem too cautious of mixing with sinners. It is not fair to blame this entirely on a hyper-Calvinistic mindset, although in some cases this is valid. The true cause is likely what was known by Andrew Fuller and William Carey as a "procrastinating spirit."[23] Like the Israelites in Haggai 1:2 who said, "The time is not come, the time the Lord's house should be built," many Reformed believers are likewise slow to undertake "any great or good work for the cause of Christ."[24] Our obsession with being doctrinally sound means that everything has to be precise and certain or we will never act. As noble as this is, it can also be debilitating. Fuller points out that because Martin Luther never had such a procrastinating spirit, he was able to undertake "the glorious work of the Reformation," otherwise the Lord's house might have been "lain waste to this day."[25]

---

[22] Charles H. Spurgeon, "The Great Sin of Doing Nothing," Christian Classics Ethereal Library, 1886, Vol. 32, No. 1916, 1886, https://www.ccel.org/ccel/spurgeon/sermons32.xl.html.

[23] Haykin, *The Missionary Fellowship of William Carey*, 55.

[24] Haykin, *The Missionary Fellowship of William Carey*, 55.

[25] Haykin, *The Missionary Fellowship of William Carey*, 55.

In a real sense, evangelism is about storming the gates of hell, even if it is reckless or at times without premeditation. Procrastinating until everything is just right typically dampens evangelism zeal, because things will never be "just right." There will always be some excuse. Fuller wondered "whether it was this tendency to procrastinate that had resulted in 'so few and so feeble efforts' being 'made for the propagation of the gospel in the world.'"[26] This is not to say evangelism cannot be planned or prepared, but it does mean that at the end of the day, evangelism is the simple duty to "go, therefore" (Matt. 28:19), which requires us to leave the confines of the church, study, and conferences, and to get our hands messy in the battle.

Most Reformed Christians believe that "God's intention for the local congregation of believers is that it be an aggressive evangelistic body, seeking 'to enlighten the whole earth'" with the gospel.[27] But the practical output of such a mindset seems to be missing: "Some who claim to possess a more precise theology of evangelism do nothing to win sinners to Christ. Absence of evangelistic zeal is a dreadful predicament."[28] It is observed that "some who demonstrate a passion for accurate doctrine, place a question mark over their love for God by evidencing no active love for lost sinners. This absence of missionary effort is appalling."[29] We would never allow Finney-ism or decisionism to come into our churches, but what are we doing when it comes to the lost? Jeremy Walker notices the same trend: "Our problems perhaps do not lie so much in

---

[26] Haykin, *The Missionary Fellowship of William Carey*, 56.

[27] Haykin, *The Missionary Fellowship of William Carey*, 53.

[28] Walter J. Chantry, *Today's Gospel* (Carlisle, PA: The Banner of Truth, 1970), 15.

[29] Chantry, *Today's Gospel*, 24.

the things that we would do but in the things that we are not doing as individuals and churches."[30]

This is not meant to be a calloused rebuke of the Reformed church. Reformed Christianity has done more for the advancement of Christ's kingdom than any other group or denomination. But we are far from achieving the goal. Now is the time to be honest with ourselves. Is there evangelistic zeal in most Reformed churches? Are the perishing millions taken seriously? In our individual lives, do we commit ourselves to teaching the lost about Christ? Say what we want about Arminians and cults and radical Calvinists, most of them could answer these questions in the affirmative. Using the analogy of a fit lifeguard on the side of a pool, Walker exhorts,

> This is neither the time for smugness and criticism from the lean lifeguards as they stand on the side sneering at the dog-paddling—the awkward but effective splashing—of those who do not know how to swim like us, nor the moment to complain about the state of the pool, still less to criticize harshly those who are drowning for getting themselves into trouble in the first place. Now is the time to jump into the filthy water and do all in our power to bring drowning people to safety.[31]

At the essence of Romans 9, one of the most illuminating texts in all of Scripture when it comes to predestination, Paul's heart breaks for the reprobate: "I have great sorrow and unceasing anguish in my heart. For I could wish that I myself

---

[30] Jeremy Walker, *The Brokenhearted Evangelist* (Grand Rapids, MI: Reformation Heritage Books, 2012), 80.

[31] Walker, *The Brokenhearted Evangelist*, 81.

were accursed and cut off from Christ for the sake of my brothers, my kinsmen according to the flesh" (Rom. 9:2-3). In the next chapter, rather than excusing their damnation or dismissing them as already predestined to judgment, he says "my heart's desire and prayer to God for them is that they may be saved" (Rom. 10:1). He goes on to give us the means of their salvation, if it is to take place: "And how are they to hear without someone preaching?...So faith comes from hearing, and hearing through the word of Christ" (Rom. 10:14-17). Paul's high view of God's sovereignty does not keep him bound within the confines of the church or the study. It motivates him to go out that the lost might hear and be saved.

Some unbelievers will reject the gospel. Others, according to God's election, will believe. When we share the gospel, people are either going to be saved or they are not, but it still takes us sharing it. Reformed Christians would agree with this. By and large, however, many of us are simply not willing to do this. It is relatively easy to study books, to be sound in doctrine, to practice a regulative principle of worship, to catechize our families at home, and to attend all the Bible studies. It is easy to live a sterilized and insulated Reformed Christianity. Sadly, most of our churches are filled with such Christians. Such a Christianity will receive little persecution or ire of man. Everything is neat and tidy. We are intellectually sound and acute. We have our comfortable niches in the church. But once our theology is taken into the world, everything changes. Once we leave the comfort of our books and living rooms and engage the culture with the gospel, suddenly we are a stench of death. We are no longer respected or considered intelligent. We realize the lost don't care about church order or John Calvin. We realize we are the scum of the earth. In church, among other Reformed Christians, we are safe and respected. But hiding behind our church attendance and catechism is no replacement for gospel proclamation to the lost. It is no excuse for saying we have done our duties as Christians. While by no means discrediting studying, catechizing, church attendance, or the regulative principle of worship, this is not all that has been commanded of us, whether or not we are leaders in the church. We are told to take the gospel to the lost. Writing about such tendencies, Walker says,

> It is too easy to assume a bunker mentality with regard to the local church. We try to keep the world at bay and perhaps assume that within the hermetically sealed confines of the congregation we can preserve ourselves intact without needing to come into contact with the world. But we cannot breed Christians by natural means.... We cannot fill the church through a breeding program, and God has not called us to do so...It we want our churches to be faithful, thriving, growing churches, it must happen through the conversion of sinners.[32]

If the Reformed Christian alone can evangelize in a consistently Biblical way, why are we so far behind in eagerness? The Reformed Christian has historically been the first to lead the charge in matters of evangelism, so why is evangelism today led by Arminians and cults? The procrastinating spirit is a real phenomenon in Reformed circles, and it is the opposite mindset of Paul and the other apostles: "It would be a gross

---

[32] Walker, *The Brokenhearted Evangelist*, 31-32.

mistake to suppose that the apostles sat down and worked out a plan of campaign: the spread of Christianity was, as we have seen, largely accompanied by informal missionaries, and must have been to a large extent haphazard and spontaneous."[33]

Morton Smith comments on this troubling trend in *Reformed Evangelism*: "All too often the man who has come to an awareness of the truth of the Reformed faith, has not thought through the implications of that faith in terms of evangelism."[34] R.B. Kuiper observes that the Reformed church does not "invade the world" with the gospel. It has lost the militant mindset which the historic church always had: "Perhaps they insist that only the pure Word of God be preached from their pulpits, but they fail to proclaim the true gospel to the lost. They would build up saints in the faith, but they do not seek to persuade the unsaved to faith. Priding themselves on their orthodoxy, they are afflicted with orthodoxism. Such churches are slumbering."[35]

Sometimes we have to just plunge into battle, without overthinking things. This is not to say we should be careless or undiscerning, but it is to say that we must do everything in our strength to get the gospel to the people, regardless of what it takes. And if we don't, the Arminians and cults will continue to be the champions of evangelism, as is evidenced in our towns, cities, and around the world. So what should we do about it? Where do we go from here? The next section will continue to address these questions.

---

[33] Michael Green, *Evangelism in the Early Church* (Grand Rapids, MI: W. B. Eerdmans, 1970), 256.

[34] Morton H. Smith, *Reformed Evangelism* (Clinton, MS: Multi-Communication Ministries, 1975), 14.

[35] R.B. Kuiper, *God-Centered Evangelism* (Carlisle, PA: The Banner of Truth, 1966), 54-55.

CHAPTER 4

Evangelism & Apologetics[1]

APOLOGETICS AND EVANGELISM go hand in hand. Apologetics, or defending the faith (1 Peter 3:15), will always be necessary when evangelizing. This is because evangelism is an intentional effort to expose the inconsistency of another person's worldview or belief system, while at the same time demonstrating the consistency of what the Scriptures teach and proclaim.

Every Christian should make a serious, self-conscious effort to become better prepared to "make a defense to anyone who asks you for a reason for the hope that is in you," and to do so in a way that presents Christ as set apart or sanctified as Lord God in your hearts (1 Peter 3:15). Every Christian must "contend" for the faith (Phil. 1:7, Jude 3) as he is given opportunity. Apologetics is not only for the specialized theologian

---

[1] Some sections of this chapter have been developed from *A Certain Sound: A Primer on Open Air Preaching*, written by Scott Smith and myself (Grand Rapids, MI: Reformation Heritage Books, 2019).

or minister. It is not something that only academic or elite
Christians do. It is something every Christian does any time
biblical evangelism takes place, whether or not the Christian
is aware of it. Here too a biblical approach is critical. There are
many schools or methods of apologetics these days, but not all
of them are faithful to the Scriptures.

This chapter will argue for a presuppositional approach
when it comes to apologetics and evangelism, which is a dis-
tinctively Reformed apologetic that begins and ends with the
God of the Scriptures and which is in accordance with the
demand to set Christ apart as Lord over everything we do,
including apologetics.[2] "It assumes Christianity's truth at the
outset and then challenges the natural man by demonstrating
that on his presuppositions nothing is true, nothing can be
accounted for, and his own thinking is invalid."[3] Presuppositional apologetics aims to demonstrate that Christianity is the
only valid worldview that exists, and it is impossible for it to
not be true.

The Impossibility of Neutrality

When evangelizing, unbelievers will pose many questions
and criticisms regarding Christianity. As Greg Bahnsen notes,
"The resistance may be emotional (ridicule, disdain, apathy)
or behavioral (living disobediently, refusing to give thanks or
offer worship), but sometimes it is intellectual."[4] The Chris-

---

[2] Cornelius Van Til, Greg Bahnsen, Gordon Clark and Francis Schaeffer are typically considered
the leading presuppositional apologists, although the tradition began much earlier with John
Calvin, Augustine, and most importantly with the authors of Scripture.

[3] Rousas John Rushdoony, *By What Standard* (Vallecito, CA: Ross House, 1995), 100.

[4] Greg Bahnsen, *Van Til's Apologetic* (Phillipsburg, N.J.: P&R Publishing, 1998), 699–700.

tian should endeavor to answer each of these challenges in a way that points to the gospel. Just as importantly, his answer must be consistent with the convictions of biblical orthodoxy. The Christian must never assume that neutral ground exists between a believer and an unbeliever, nor that the unbeliever is unbiased or open-minded, especially in light of biblical revelation. Unbelievers are hostile to God (Eph. 4:17-18). By nature, unbelievers are children of wrath (Eph. 2:3). Even if they follow some other kind of religion, it is merely an "exchange" of "the glory of the immortal God" with a god or idol who does not exist (Rom. 1:23).

This is the problem with evidential and classical approaches to apologetics, which assume that the unbeliever is open-minded or merely lacking correct information about God. These approaches present evidence for the existence of God or some other Christian truth claim to the unbeliever, who then sits in the place of a judge, evaluating the evidence. God's existence is on trial. Maybe it is the historical reliability of Jesus or the resurrection or the virgin birth. The unbeliever goes on to determine that the evidence is lacking. Or, granting that the evidence is persuasive, the unbeliever goes on to say he still needs more evidence. If nothing else, the unbeliever will go home and do research to justify himself against the argument just put forward by the Christian, which means the Christian must then arm himself with further arguments to combat this new evidence. This cycle will then be repeated over and over since the problem is not a lack of evidence, but rather how such evidence is interpreted.

Unbelievers are biased against God. They will always interpret evidence in a way that justifies their rebellion against God and love of sin. They will always act in accordance with the "vanity of their mind" (Eph. 4:17), whose thoughts are always against God (Col. 1:21). What the unbeliever needs is a new mind, not new evidence. He needs the new birth, not new arguments about God.

Unbelievers Always Aim at Preserving Their Autonomy

When evangelizing, we are dealing with unbelievers whose worldview assumes that the human mind has ultimate authority. The unbeliever will make himself the reference point for interpreting reality and will subordinate God's Word to his own autonomous (self-rule, self-law) reasoning, which is at war with God. The Christian must show that reality is what God says it is in Scripture. God is the one who shows us how to correctly interpret reality, since He is its creator, sustainer, and governor. All human knowledge must be subordinated to that plan. This is why no neutral ground exists between the believer and the unbeliever. All ground belongs to Christ. The natural man must always borrow from Christ's universe even to deny His existence.

The Christian must labor to show that the unbeliever's worldview will always be untenable or inconsistent with what he or she claims to believe. The Christian must then turn the tables by pointing out that, in contrast, Christianity is the only worldview consistent with what it claims. The unbeliever must be shown that his worldview cannot make sense of reality without borrowing from Christian presuppositions. For instance, logic, science, mathematics, morality, and other disciplines cannot be valid or justified unless grounded on the objective, eternal, unchangeable God of the Bible. Likewise, any interpretation of reality must be thoroughly Christian if it is to be accurate or consistent, since Christ has made all things and is the only way man's redemption is possible. For an unbeliever to say he can know anything at all is impossible unless the triune God of the Bible is the reason for it. Truth is that which conforms to the mind of God as known through Christ (Col. 2:3; John 1:9).

Do Atheists and Agnostics Actually Exist?

Professing atheists and agnostics deny the need for any form of divine authority. Unbelievers worship the supposed autonomy of human reason, whether their own or some other "qualified" authority. This could include their professor, their parents, a television show or book, or "science." This is their attempt to suppress the truth of God. This is why any concept of authority that is outside the human mind will be unacceptable to them.

But the Bible teaches that no such thing as an actual atheist or agnostic exists. Consider Romans 1, for instance. Paul, in the original Greek text, describes the unbelieving man as "knowing *the* God" (v. 21), which implies an intellectual awareness of God. The definite article proves it is not a vague or abstract awareness of some God or deity but the very God of the universe. This does not mean they know that God is triune or that He has made a way for our sins to be remedied. It does mean, however, that they are aware of the God who created and sustains the universe.

Most Christian apologists attempt to argue for some version of God or deity. They assume that if they can get the unbeliever to admit of the existence of a God, then gradually they will come to believe in *the* God. But a god is different than the true God, so this approach is dishonest. The Bible shows that the unbeliever already has knowledge of God, which is why Paul can say "because" (v. 21) men have this knowledge, they are "without an excuse," or literally "without an apologetic" or "defense" for their unrighteous and reprobate living (vv. 20, 23–31). Their thanklessness (v. 21) and foolish thinking (vv. 21–22) are not done in ignorance. God's wrath justly rests on all persons outside of Christ because He has manifested Himself to them in such a way that they know "that which may be known of God" (v. 19). Whether someone lives in the jungles of South America or in urbanized China, they clearly see enough of God's divine attributes to render them accountable to God (v. 20). Every human without exception knows "the truth of God" (v. 25). But unbelievers do not deem it worthwhile to "retain God in their knowledge" (v. 28), choosing rather to suppress the truth by means of their unrighteousness (v. 18).

Paul is claiming that the unbeliever has definite beliefs about God and possesses full and overwhelming "proof" for those beliefs. This is why there is no such thing as a genuine atheist or agnostic and why it is nearly always a wasted effort to give evidence for God's existence rather than call for the unbeliever to repent of his supposed autonomy and submit to the evidence he already has.[5] This can be done by pointing out the inconsistency of so-called autonomous reasoning.

Again, the unbeliever's problem or lack of belief is due to

---

[5] Greg Bahnsen influences much of the language here.

his heart, not evidence. His problem is his hatred for God. He hates the existence of God and His written revelation. He hates the idea that God is King of the universe. The unbeliever is actively at war against God, whether or not he admits it. Since the time the unbeliever came "from the womb" (Ps. 58:3), he has been living in rebellion against God, so naturally he has an axe to grind against him.

Denying God's existence or other truth claims of Scripture is a defense mechanism to quiet the conscience. It is an attempt to sin boldly without any regard for the Judge of the universe. But he does regard this Judge. The unbeliever knows that every square inch of the universe testifies to His reality. This is why the unbeliever does everything in his power to suppress such truth. Consider Van Til's remarks: "Men ought, says Calvin following Paul, to believe in God, for each one is surrounded with a super-abundance of evidence with respect to him. The whole universe is lit up by God. Scripture requires men to accept its interpretation of history as true without doubt. Doubt of this kind...is as unreasonable as a child asking whether he has parents and, after looking at the evidence, concluding that he probably has."[6]

All people have a personal worldview or commitment that acts as chief authority in their life. This is what the Christian must drive home and expose when evangelizing. An unbeliever's authority will be himself or some other mistake-prone human, and it will always prove inconsistent with what it claims. Ever since Adam ate the forbidden fruit, men have tried to make themselves God. Naturally hostile in mind toward God (1 Cor. 1:21), they consider themselves to be the ultimate criterion of

---

[6] Cornelius Van Til, *The Reformed Pastor and Modern Thought* (Nutley, N.J.: Presbyterian and Reformed, 1971), 32–34.

truth and set themselves up as knowing the universe better than God. They reference everything in light of their own reason or desire, which of course is debilitated by sin. Adam and Eve did the same thing when they bit into the fruit, but without God as a reference, how can the unbeliever be certain his reason is even valid? How can he assume to know anything at all? How can reason, knowledge, truth, and consciousness come from inert, lifeless, truth-less material? This is the folly of making one's self the standard of truth. It always proves to be inconsistent with reality.

The Only Hope for Meaning and Rationality Is Christ

The rational man, the moral man, and the scientific man all operate on the assumption that the ultimate reference point is the human being. As Bahnsen notes, the Christian must show that the ultimate source of truth in any field is found in Christ alone: "The fact of science and its progress is inexplicable except upon the presupposition that the world is made and controlled by God through Christ and that man is made and renewed in the image of God through Christ."[7] It is impossible for the unbeliever to account for science, logic, morality, uniformity in the universe, or any other law or fact apart from Christ. Biblical apologetics demonstrates to the unbeliever the irrationality and even impossibility of all other worldviews other than historic Christianity: "The way to prove the truth of Christianity, then, is to take the conflicting worldviews of the Christian and the non-Christian—with their opposing presuppositions and theories of knowledge, in terms of

---

[7] Bahnsen, *Van Til's Apologetic*, 710.

which particular claims are disputed back and forth—and press for a critical internal analysis of each one, looking for philosophical inconsistency and absurdity. This is the way to refute the unbeliever's bedrock presuppositions, showing the intellectual impossibility of any worldview that is contrary to Christianity."[8]

Meaning can be accounted for only by God's Word, apart from which the capacity to reason would be impossible. God is the reason for objective, unchangeable laws in the universe, such as logic or truth. God's knowledge of the universe is exhaustive because He is the creator and sustainer of it. Thus, God must be the chief authority for everything we do because everything begins with and continues through Him. And more specifically, the written revelation of this God must be the source by which everything else is to be evaluated.

The unbeliever always uses his God-given reasoning capacity to make any claim concerning that same God, even if it is to deny His existence. Without an acknowledgment of God, the unbeliever is forced to say he knows his reasoning is valid because his reasoning makes it so. But his reasoning powers are subject to mistakes. They are far from omniscient. The Christian knows his reasoning is valid because it conforms to an objective, unchangeable source—the triune God—and His written revelation, the Scriptures.

Without belief in the God of Scripture, it is impossible for the unbeliever to prove anything at all, not only in religion but also in logic, science, experience, history, or morality: "This is what is meant by the 'presuppositional method' of defending

---

[8] Bahnsen, *Van Til's Apologetic*, 701.

the faith. It calls upon the unbeliever to confess his intellectual rebellion and ruin, and then to submit in faith, thanksgiving, and obedience to the claims of the self-attesting Christ."[9]

Man Is Always in Need of God's Special Revelation

The Scriptures must be the ultimate criterion of truth for every Christian, and no less so when doing apologetics. Many Christians claim that the Bible is the ultimate criterion for truth but then compromise when defending or contending for the faith. They will take a more "neutral" position when it comes to revelation. As Bahnsen notes, a Christian must stand on the authority of the Bible in every aspect of his life, which includes dealing with unbelievers: "Since sin has come into the world, God's interpretation of the facts must come in finished, written form and be comprehensive in character. God continues to reveal himself in the facts of the created world, but the sinner needs to interpret every one of them in the clearer light of Scripture. Every thought on every subject must become obedient to the requirement of God as he speaks in his Word; every thought must be brought into subjection to Christ."[10]

Ever since God spoke to Adam in paradise before the fall, He has used supernatural communication to deal with His people.[11] This is the case even though sinners, apart from the Holy Spirit, will always attempt to eradicate God's Word. Biblical apologetics does not ask the unbeliever to consider the possibility of the Bible's authority. This again is the dif-

---

[9] Bahnsen, *Van Til's Apologetic*, 701.

[10] Bahnsen, *Van Til's Apologetic*, 70–71.

[11] "The Bible is the supernatural communication of God to creatures who have become sinners."
    Bahnsen, *Van Til's Apologetic*, 713.

ference between biblical apologetics and more traditional or evidential approaches. It begins with the Bible as self-authoritative and self-attesting, and it claims that without such revelation, no meaningful interpretation of anything could be possible. Christ as God speaks in the Bible with absolute authority. Thus, the Bible does not appeal to human reason for its justification, otherwise humans would be positioned as more authoritative than God's Word. Rather, the Bible comes to the human being with absolute authority and demands that men submit to it.

Circular Reasoning?

Some criticize the presuppositional approach as being a viciously circular argument since it begins with the Bible as self-authoritative and self-attesting. These critics fail to understand that every argument about ultimate authorities must in some sense be "circular." If you are arguing with an unbeliever about the existence of God or the truth claims of Christianity, he will tell you they are wrong because he says they are wrong. The unbeliever may appeal to something outside of himself to make that claim, but he will be the one who judges the evidence to be more authoritative than the Bible. In other words, he begins with himself as the ultimate authority and assumes it is self-attesting. When pressed, he will be forced to admit that the "evidence" about God's existence or other truth claims found in Scripture is judged to be lacking, just because he says so. His argument circles around himself. Even if he brings in the writings or evidence from some historian or scientist to validate his point, he still must make the judgment that the historian or scientist is more reliable than the Bible. Thus, his own reason will always be the reference point. Ironically, however, in order to make arguments against the Bible, he must assume things about the world that are true only because the God who wrote the Bible has made them true.

But the Christian must never give up the Bible as the ultimate reference point in evangelism, because nothing is more authoritative than God's Word. God Himself appeals to Himself as the ultimate authority (Heb. 6:16), since to appeal to anything else would make that thing more authoritative than God. Anything that is inconsistent with the Bible is wrong because the Bible, as God's revelation, is always the ultimate authority, not man. The Bible as God's revelation is sufficient, infallible, and inerrant since it comes from an eternal, perfect Being who created and sustains the universe.

Van Til deals with this charge of circular reasoning in several of his works: "Now if it be called circular reasoning when we hold it necessary to presuppose the existence of God, we are not ashamed of it because we are firmly convinced that all forms of reasoning that leave God out of account will end in ruin."[12] Or consider again his remarks on the inspiration of Scripture: "The only alternative to 'circular reasoning' as engaged in by Christians, no matter on what point they speak, is that of reasoning on the basis of isolated facts and isolated minds, with the result that there is no possibility of reasoning at all."[13] This is because man is sinful and profoundly limited in our understanding of reality. Our interpretation of the

---

[12] Van Til, as quoted in Bahnsen, *Van Til's Apologetic*, 519.

[13] Cornelius Van Til, *An Introduction to Systematic Theology* (Nutley, N.J.: Presbyterian and Reformed, 1974), 43.

universe will always be faulty and biased toward sinful men, which is why specific revelation is necessary. "Unless as sinners we have an absolutely inspired Bible, we have no absolute God interpreting reality for us, and unless we have an absolute God interpreting reality for us, there is no true interpretation at all."[14]

Circular reasoning in the sense of ultimate authority is not fallacious, therefore. Starting with the Bible as self-authoritative and self-attesting is in no way some kind of lesser or invalid form of presentation. Everyone uses an ultimate authority for making a case. Presuppositional apologetics rightly posits that the only options on the table are God's revelation or man's reason. But only God's revelation can be held as authoritative without inconsistency or error: "The only alternative to starting with the 'I AM' of Christ is to start with the 'I am' of man in some such way.... Thus false circular reasoning stands over against true circular reasoning."[15]

To consider this from another perspective, "the circular argument uses its own conclusion as one of its stated or unstated premises. Instead of offering proof, it simply asserts the conclusion in another form, thereby inviting the listener to accept it as settled when, in fact, it has not been settled."[16] This is not what presuppositional apologetics is doing when it comes to biblical authority. On the contrary, presuppositional apologetics demonstrates that Scripture's self-authenticity can be verified by the truth of what it claims to be, as well as its

---

[14] Cornelius Van Til, *An Introduction to Systematic Theology*, 43.

[15] Cornelius Van Til, *Christianity in Conflict* (Philadelphia: Westminster Theological Seminary, 1962–1964 (syllabus), chap. 9.

[16] T. Edward Damer, *Attacking Faulty Reasoning* (Belmont, CA: Wadsworth, 2001).

other inherent marks of divinity. The Westminster Confession's statement on the Bible will help here:

> And the heavenliness of the matter, the efficacy of the doctrine, the majesty of the style, the consent of all the parts, the scope of the whole (which is, to give all glory to God), the full discovery it makes of the only way of man's salvation, the many other incomparable excellencies, and the entire perfection thereof, are arguments whereby it doth abundantly evidence itself to be the Word of God: yet notwithstanding, our full persuasion and assurance of the infallible truth and divine authority thereof, is from the inward work of the Holy Spirit bearing witness by and with the Word in our hearts.[17]

Such marks of Scripture's divinity do not make the Bible self-authenticating. Rather, because the Bible is self-authenticating, it contains such marks. It is entirely consistent with what we would expect a revelation from God to contain.

Cults and World Religions

Presuppositional apologetics can be used to challenge other religious faiths as well. The approach would be no different from confronting atheism. The Christian must internally examine whatever worldview is being presented from the viewpoint of that religion. By doing so, it will become evident that contradictions exist between what a person claims to believe, and how that claim actually matches up to reality. Religions that stem from or have been influenced by the Bible, such as

---

[17] The Westminster Confession of Faith (1647), I.v.

Islam, Mormonism, or Jehovah's Witnesses, can be treated as Christian heresies and reasoned against by using Scripture itself to show where they have departed from the truth.

Although it is helpful to have an understanding of other religions and cults when defending or contending for the faith, it is just as useful to have a grasp of biblical doctrine and church history. Being able to clearly articulate orthodox doctrine or certain contexts of church history will be useful against most world religions or cults, which are usually by-products if not duplications of prior heretical movements.[18] Knowledge of church history will help the Christian identify such heresies and know how the Christians of old defended the faith against them. This is why the Christian would best spend his time studying doctrine and church history rather than evidential arguments for the existence of God or other Christian truth claims. He would also benefit from studying the specific religions or cults he is likely to engage, which includes Darwinian evolution, Marxism, militant veganism, and other groups that would deny being explicitly "religious."

The Christian must also be sensitive to sincere questions when evangelizing the lost, as opposed to those intended to stump him. Like Satan, the unbeliever will often twist the Scriptures in an attempt to make the Christian contradict himself. Spending time with such persons could be an example of casting "pearls before swine" (Matt. 7:6), although this is not always the case. When encountering someone who is sincerely wrestling or having difficulty with some doctrine of the faith, such as the resurrection or the virgin birth, using

---

[18] This includes Islam and even Marxism, both of which are spin-offs in many ways of orthodox Christianity.

Scripture instead of classical or evidential approaches is advised, since there is no higher authority than Scripture. As Greg Bahnsen explains,

> Traditional evidentialism does not handle the evidence as it should. It pretends that there are neutral facts or neutral methods for examining the facts.... In every presentation of a factual argument for Christianity, the defender of the faith is implicitly—if not explicitly—challenging the unbeliever with an entire system or Christian worldview of which the fact is a part. "Facts" do not stand outside of systems of thought, as though they could help us to choose among them. In any factual argument, whether attention is drawn to it or not, two worldviews are set next to each other for comparison.[19]

The Holy Spirit and Apologetics

The Christian must constantly be seeking wisdom from the Holy Spirit. Each apologetic encounter will be different, but the aim must be the command to call upon the name of the Lord Jesus to be saved. The goal is not necessarily to prove God or the Bible, nor should it be to win an argument. The Christian must show that all men are without excuse for their unbelief, and that any claim or position that is inconsistent with the Scriptures is not only incorrect but can be demonstrated to be so.

At the end of the day, only the Holy Spirit can give faith to the unbeliever, but we are called on to present God's truth in a biblical, Christ-centered way. This is why the presuppositional

---

[19] Bahnsen, *Van Til's Apologetic*, 641.

approach to defending the faith is preferred to any other. Even R. C. Sproul, an opponent of presuppositional apologetics, admits "the existence of God is the supreme *proto*-supposition for all theoretical thought. God's existence is the chief element in constructing any worldview. To deny this chief premise is to set one's sails for the island of nihilism. This is the darkest continent of the darkened mind—the ultimate paradise of the fool."[20] This is what a Christian must be eager to expose and why he must make a concerted effort to better contend for and defend the faith in a biblical, God-honoring manner, and in such a way that is precise (Acts 18:26).

---

[20] R. C. Sproul, *The Consequences of Ideas: Understanding the Concepts that Shaped our World* (Wheaton, Ill.: Crossway, 2000), 171.

PART TWO

RIGHT PRACTICE

CHAPTER 5

The Foolishness of God

WHEN EVANGELISM IS LEFT UP TO MAN, the options we have for subduing the wills of others are eloquent reasoning, force of arms, or worldly attractions. But Jesus prohibits "force of arms" when it comes to evangelism. Paul dismantles the eloquent reasoning approach in 1 Corinthians 1-2. Worldly attraction is nowhere condoned or exemplified by the New Testament disciples. And yet, these last two approaches are exactly the kind used most in modern evangelism. John Owen reminds us that such options "were abandoned" by the early Christians, "and they declared against the use of them.... Persuasive orations, enticing words, alluring arts and eloquence, with the like effects of human wisdom and skill, were all of them studiously declined by them in this work."[1] The early church knew of only one way to evangelize, regardless of its

---

[1] John Owen, *The Work of the Spirit* (Carlisle, PA: The Banner of Truth Trust: 1967), 39.

results: "This alone they betook themselves unto—they went up and down, preaching to Jews and Gentiles 'that Jesus Christ died for our sins, and rose again, according to the Scriptures.'"[2]

Owen tells us that such an approach "was looked on as a marvelous foolish thing, a sweaty kind of babbling, by all those who had got any reputation of learning or cunning amongst men."[3] What is more, such an approach to evangelism "was under as many improbabilities of success, unto all rational conjectures, as can be conceived." Paul "knew what the Jews wanted—signs. He knew what the Greeks wanted—wisdom. What was his response? He preached a crucified Messiah.... He didn't give them what they wanted or felt they needed. Paul instead chose to give them what Christ had said they needed."[4]

Most modern evangelism does not go about it in this way. Unlike the early church, most Christians today are at odds with the notion that "God's power does not rely upon programs, methods, or resources; it does not rely on hiring a dynamic speaker, someone with a PhD, or being culturally 'relevant.' God's power and wisdom are found in the gospel."[5] What is more, many modern Christians criticize those who believe that the simple gospel is enough, especially since it causes the same disturbance in our culture as it did in the days of the early church:

> No sooner did the rulers and governors of the world begin to take notice of them and what they did, but they judged that it all tended to sedition, and that commotions would

---

[2] Owen, *The Work of the Spirit*, 39.
[3] Owen, *The Work of the Spirit*, 39.
[4] Joe Kohler, *The Forgotten Officer* (Bloomington, IN: WestBow Press, 2016), 60.
[5] Kohler, *The Forgotten Officer*, 60.

ensue thereon. These things enraged the generality of mankind against them and their converts; who therefore made havoc of them with incredible fury.[6]

Owen points out that such an approach to evangelism, then as now, could only produce the most disastrous consequences imaginable from a worldly point of view. Not to mention that the captain of their message "was newly crucified by the present powers of the earth for a malefactor," and they themselves were "a company of sorry craftsmen" who "were able to fill a whole city with tumult and uproar against the gospel."[7] There is no worse way to go about it, in other words. And who would deny that "the world seemed very sufficiently fortified against the admission of this new and strange doctrine, on the terms whereon it was proposed. There can be no danger, sure, that ever it should obtain any considerable progress."[8]

If the early church had been concerned with numerical success or "the one," they might have approached their circumstance much differently. They might have considered the felt needs of the population or established program-driven churches. They might have consulted sociologists and psychologists. They might have used the little resources they had to conduct surveys or hire successful business persons to teach them their secrets. They might have come up with some method, perhaps "relational" in nature, that allowed them to hide the gospel until a more convenient time became available. They might have considered how to be friendlier with the culture. Instead, they kept to the God-given methods of

---

[6] Owen, *The Work of the Spirit*, 39-40.

[7] Owen, *The Work of the Spirit*, 41.

[8] Owen, *The Work of the Spirit*, 41.

intercessory prayer and gospel proclamation, regardless of the results it produced. This alone is God's method of evangelism: "Evangelism should not manipulate the will by appealing to the sinner's natural desires. It is normal for sinners to wish for better things for themselves—like health, wealth, success, and personal fulfillment.... By contrast, the true gospel offers what is incongruous to natural human desire."[9] What is more, Owen points out that their message commanded the complete allegiance of everyone it came into contact with, which is impossible for the natural man to accept:

> Had it only been a new doctrine and religion, declaring that knowledge and worship of God which had never heard of before, they could not but be very wary in giving it entertainment; but when withal it required, at the first instant, that for its sake they should 'pull out their right eyes, and cut off their right hands,' to part with all that was dear and useful unto them, and which had such a prevalent interest in their minds and affections as corrupt lusts are known to have, this could not but invincibly fortify them against its admittance.[10]

The evangelism of the early church was not calculated to be easy to accept. It was calculated to be impossible to accept apart from the grace of God, which in turn gives Him all the glory. It was not calculated to be as pleasing as possible to the hearers, but rather the opposite. The early church was concerned with being faithful in the proclamation of the gospel, including its demands, leaving the results up to God. "And yet,

---

[9] John MacArthur, "Theology of Sleep," *Evangelism* (Nashville, TN: Thomas Nelson, 2011), 13.
[10] Owen, *The Work of the Spirit*, 42.

notwithstanding all these disadvantages, and against all these oppositions, their doctrine prevailed to subdue the world to the obedience thereof."[11] This is the fact that has always baffled secular historians and even modern Christians. God has designed evangelism to be the proclamation of an inane message by inane people, so that the wisdom of the world would be confounded. This was intentional.

When it comes to evangelism methods, Paul did the same thing in whatever city he went to: "His approach was direct, confrontive evangelism. He did not do a community survey. He did not conduct any special research. He didn't try to put together an evangelization committee. He just went to the synagogue and the marketplace and preached to whoever was there."[12] Again, "As we examine Paul's ways, we can see that he did not establish program-driven churches; he never took surveys of the felt needs of the community. We have no record of his using resources to create fun, no-strings-attached programs to appeal to the churches."[13] Yet when it comes to evangelism today, because of lack of numerical success in the realm of conversions, most Christians have stopped relying on the plain proclamation of the gospel and have instead returned to Babylon and Egypt for more impressive ideas.

The Sap of Pragmatism

Arminian Darius Salter admits that "pragmatism has meant the unceasing effort to search for methodologies that will be

---

[11] Owen, *The Work of the Spirit*, 40.

[12] John MacArthur, *Ashamed of the Gospel* (Wheaton, IL: Crossway Books, 1993), 153.

[13] Joe Kohler, *The Forgotten Officer*, 59.

numerically efficient in the great harvest of souls," which he thinks justifies its use.[14] John MacArthur defines pragmatism as "the notion that meaning or worth is determined by practical consequences."[15] In the area of evangelism, it would mean that if a method works or sees many converts, it is more valuable than a method that does not see many converts, regardless of what the Bible says about it. Proclaiming the full counsel of God to people who are lost will not be seen as very useful or effective, and so another method will be desired. MacArthur facetiously comments, "Preaching the Word and boldly confronting sin are seen as archaic, ineffectual means of winning the world. After all, those things actually drive most people away."[16] This is the mindset of pragmatic evangelism, and most of Western Christianity is dominated by it.

Finney was the most important forerunner of pragmatic evangelism, claiming that "the connection between the right use of means for a revival and a revival, is as philosophically sure as between the right use of means to raise grain and a crop of wheat. I believe, in fact, it is more certain and that there are fewer instances of failure."[17] The problem with this should be glaring. It is a production of man, not God. Its aim is numerical success, even if counterfeit. Evangelism is seen as a marketing challenge. Not everyone is ecstatic about such approaches, however: "Some speak of 'persuasion' as if the outcome could be secured by human effort, almost as if it were another word

---

[14] Darius Salter, *American Evangelism* (Grand Rapids, MI: Baker Book House, 1996), 85.

[15] MacArthur, *Ashamed of the Gospel*, 26.

[16] MacArthur, *Ashamed of the Gospel*, 32.

[17] Salter, *American Evangelism*, 95-96.

for 'coercion.' But no. Our responsibility is to be faithful; the results are in the hand of Almighty God."[18]

Iain Murray comments on how such obsessions with numbers were one of the hallmarks of the Second Great Awakening, the effects of which are still devastating churches today:

What was indisputable was that making 'conversion' a matter of instant, public decision, with ascertainable numbers immediately announced in the religious press, produced a display of repeated 'successes' on a scale never before witnessed. Numbers seen to be responding were claimed as more than sufficient evidence for the rightness of the changes in practice and teaching.[19]

This approach to evangelism has caused a downgrade in Western Christianity, seen as far back as the nineteenth century, when New York pastor James Alexander said: "The gospel is not attractive enough for people now-a-days. Ministers must bait their trap with something else. The old-fashioned topics are seldom heard."[20] This pragmatic approach to evangelism is why the church's "true authority and strength" was eventually sapped: "In the end, while evangelicalism was seeking to guard faith in Scripture, it was her readiness to be impressed by pragmatic arguments, and by alleged success, by quantity rather than quality, that did so much to deprive her of true authority and strength."[21] We are told by a first-hand witness that the same thing plagued the 1904-5 Welsh Revival: "So great was the passion for results that men forgot

---

[18] John Stott, *Christian Mission in the Modern World* (Downers Grove, IL: InterVarsity Press, 2008), 87.

[19] Iain H. Murray, *Revival & Revivalism* (Carlisle, PA: The Banner of Truth, 1994), 283.

[20] Murray, *Revival & Revivalism*, 337.

[21] Murray, *Revival & Revivalism*, 383.

what was due to reverence and even to decency.... It is possible to sacrifice too much for the sake of results, and such results are seldom enduring."[22]

Ernest C. Reisinger goes even further, stating that the reason why the church is so carnal today is because people are "forever rushing on the contemporary scene with some new method while the real problem is in the message," and specifically, the message delivered at the evangelism stage, which leads to false converts.[23] And for the genuine converts who are saved in spite of such approaches, not because of them, they see their own conversion as a reason to continue using the unbiblical methods when they themselves evangelize. Rather than consult their Bible to determine how to evangelize, they rely on tradition and doing things for the sake of "the one," regardless of how they must get it: "Considering how important it is not to 'let the fish get away,' whole manuals have been written for 'successful fishing'.... The me-centered evangelist turns into a sales-person, creating undue psychological pressure."[24]

What About Hell?

In many Christian circles, including among the Reformed, there is an unspoken belief that we must tone down all mention of hell or future judgment when talking to the lost. Formally, many Christians would say they believe in hell. But when it comes to evangelism, many would say that to speak much of hell is an ineffective if not harmful approach. The

---

[22] J. Vyrnwy Morgan, *The Welsh Religious Revival*, 1904-5: A Retrospect and a Criticism (London, 1909), 140.

[23] Ernest C. Reisinger, *Today's Evangelism* (Philipsburg, NJ: Craig Press, 1982), 30.

[24] Will Metzger, *Tell the Truth* (Downers Grove, IL: InterVarsity, 1981), 122.

term "fire and brimstone" is used today in a pejorative sense, even by Christians, even though two centuries ago it was a common topic of preaching, whether in church or to the lost. There is a tacit belief that preaching on hell and judgment does not work in a culture as sophisticated as ours. But Tertullian, writing around 200 AD, shows that the same ridicule and scorn regarding hell was cast upon Christians in his day too: "We get ourselves laughed at for proclaiming that God will one day judge the world, though, like us, poets and philosophers set up a judgment seat in the world below. And if we threaten Gehenna, a reservoir of secret fire under the earth for purposes of punishment, we have derision heaped upon us."[25]

This implies that the Christians were speaking about hell in their evangelism, regardless of the "derision heaped upon" them by the culture. Also, nowhere in the writings of the early church is there any mention of Christians advising a more soft-peddled approach to topics such as hell in order to accommodate such a "sophisticated" culture as theirs. Christians are never seen arguing that people in their day are different than those in the Old Testament times, and so another strategy should be advised. This goes back to the modern church's obsession for "the one" to be saved at the expense of biblical evangelism, and also the belief that for the one to be saved, the gospel must be presented in an attractive and inoffensive fashion.

When it comes to speaking about hell, too many Christians act like Peter whenever the Jews came from Jerusalem and Paul had to rebuke him (Gal. 2:11-21). Peter acted one way with one group, but differently with another. Christians have

---

no problem admitting the realities of hell with other Christians, but when it comes to the lost, they no longer have such confidence. Many times the Christian will take the side of the lost, believing it a shameful thing for hell to be mentioned in so plain and bold a manner. Many believe that hell should be silenced altogether until "the right" time. But when did talking about hell to the lost become so taboo? When did Christians become so ashamed of hell?

John MacArthur gives some alarming examples of this. He agrees that "God's wrath is almost entirely missing from modern presentations of the gospel. It is not fashionable to speak of God's wrath against sin or to tell people they should fear God."[26] Elsewhere he says: "The typical presentation today starts exactly opposite where Paul started. He wrote of 'the wrath of God...against all ungodliness and unrighteousness of men.' But modern evangelism begins with, "God loves you and wants to make you happy."[27] MacArthur even likens evangelism that deliberately removes any mention of hell or the wrath of God to heresy: "Rather than arousing fear of God, it attempts to portray Him as fun, jovial, easygoing, lenient, and even permissive. Haughty sinners who ought to approach God in terror (cf. Luke 18:13) are emboldened to presume on His grace. Sinners hear nothing of divine wrath. That is as wrong as preaching rank heresy."[28] MacArthur notes that downplaying God's wrath or hell "does not enhance evangelism; it undermines it."[29] He then provides sobering statistics from a

---

[26] MacArthur, *Ashamed of the Gospel*, 143.
[27] MacArthur, *Ashamed of the Gospel*, 143.
[28] MacArthur, *Ashamed of the Gospel*, 75.
[29] MacArthur, *Ashamed of the Gospel*, 77.

survey given to seminary students in 1992, and we can assume the numbers would be even more troubling today: "Nearly half—46 percent—feel that preaching about hell to unbelievers is in 'poor taste.'"[30] Just as disappointing were some quotations pulled from "user-friendly churches" which describes their method of preaching. Each line represents a different church and has been extracted from a larger block of description in order to point out the specific reference to hell:

- There is no fire and brimstone here.
- You won't hear people threatened with hell or referred to as sinners.
- No ranting, no raving. No fire and brimstone. He doesn't even use the H-word.
- You won't hear a lot of preaching about sin and damnation and hell fire.
- It's a salvationist message, but the idea is not so much being saved from the fires of hell.[31]

It would be dishonest to say this problem never plagues Reformed churches or their approach to evangelism. Although Reformed churches may approach the doctrine of hell in a more biblical way, in general we are just as hesitant to speak about the "H-word" to the lost. In our attempt to reach the world, we have toned down the realities of hell, and in doing so we have abandoned our apparent allegiance to the doctrines of grace and Reformed Christianity. Some Christians omit speaking about hell for the sake of winning "the one" to Christ, but in doing so, they actually hurt their witness:

---

[30] MacArthur, *Ashamed of the Gospel*, 77.
[31] MacArthur, *Ashamed of the Gospel*, 59.

No sincere Christian intends to deceive sinners. In love
for souls, true evangelicals invariably present some pro-
found truths in their witnessing. Yet by the unconscious
omission of essential ingredients of the Gospel, many fail
to communicate even that portion of God's Word which
they mean to convey. When a half truth is presented as the
whole truth, it becomes an untruth.[32]

When it comes to evangelism, hell must be spoken of, especially considering the Bible's constant allusion to its reality and
danger. Our love for God and our love for man should drive us
to speak about it, regardless of how distasteful it is to both our
pagan and Christian cultures. Paul himself speaks of divine
wrath as one of the primary reasons for evangelism: "Therefore, knowing the fear of the Lord, we persuade others" (2 Cor.
5:11). Jesus spoke about hell more than any other person in
the Bible, including the Old Testament prophets. He warned
us to "fear him who, after the killing of the body, has power to
throw you into hell" (Lk 12:5). John, the apostle of love, tells
us, "If anyone's name was not found written in the book of life,
he was thrown into the lake of fire" (Rev. 20:15). If these men
were not ashamed to speak of hell, we should not be either.

Will Metzger notices that "our inclination to downplay the
existence of hell reflects the tendency we have to compromise
the gospel. I used to avoid mentioning hell. I didn't want to
frighten people. I was aware that people could be manipulated
and seek salvation merely as a 'fire escape.'"[33] He apparently got

---

[32] Walter J. Chantry, *Today's Gospel* (Carlisle, PA: The Banner of Truth, 1970), 17.
[33] Metzger, *Tell the Truth*, 96.

over it, saying that "part of telling the truth is reinforcing the reality and danger of hell, of which the Bible speaks clearly."[34]

We must speak of hell because it demonstrates the justice of God. Hell reveals that God is a sin-avenging judge, not the apathetic grandpa of contemporary evangelicalism. Jesus used the most horrid descriptions imaginable when it came to hell. Language fails to describe what omnipotent wrath will accomplish against the sinner in hell, yet we must do our best to communicate its realities. Rather than knocking our heads over the question about whether God could actually govern such a place as hell, it is time to take God's Word for what it is, a revelation from the God who cannot lie (Tit. 1:2), and take such a message to those who are perishing. It is contradictory for persons to be saved from hell and yet, over time, to become apathetic when it comes to trying to save others from hell themselves: "Many of us who have entered the kingdom have come perilously close to the flames of the pit. We have felt its fire, and yet we have, perhaps, forgotten that from which we have been delivered."[35] Later on Jeremy Walker asks, "If hell is the least part of what it is presented to be in God's holy Word, through those Spirit-inspired Scriptures, then how in the name and for the sake of our own humanity, let alone our Christian duty, could we ever remain silent about the truth that saves from hell?"[36] If we believe it, we are dutybound to share it. If we don't believe it, we are making God out to be a liar and are ourselves in danger of the wrath to come. There are no other options.

---

[34] Metzger, *Tell the Truth*, 96.

[35] Jeremy Walker, *The Brokenhearted Evangelist* (Grand Rapids, MI: Reformation Heritage Books, 2012), x.

[36] Walker, *The Brokenhearted Evangelist*, 35.

CHAPTER 6

The Lost Art of Scandal

WHEN IT COMES TO EVANGELISM, things are not getting easier in the West. The culture's hatred of biblical Christianity is becoming more pronounced. Yet the church is oftentimes ashamed or offended by the righteous scandal that evangelism provokes. If the church is upset now whenever evangelism causes an offense, what will happen when things get even worse? As we will see, however, God actually uses the suffering and scandal brought about by bold evangelism to attract unbelievers to the gospel in a way that pragmatic and man-pleasing approaches never could.

When the early church was taking root, there were no critiques when it came to divisive evangelism. The evangelism of the early church was explosive. It was bold. It was frontline and direct. Yet no one within the church is ever seen condemning it. There was never a meeting among the elders to discuss whether they should go about evangelizing in such a brash manner, especially considering the persecution and even martyrdom that it often caused. People not only lost jobs but houses as well (Heb. 10:34). People were harried from city to city, as well as stoned and crucified. Yet no one in the Christian community ever questions the "efficacy" of such an approach. In fact, we can consider such silence on the matter to be an indication that such an approach to evangelism was normal and even proper in the eyes of the early church. Nowhere in the Acts of the Apostles or anywhere else in the New Testament do we have a hint that "the Apostles or Early Church martyrs were ever faulted or condemned by their brothers in Christ."[1]

To illustrate this, consider Paul's approach to evangelism while in Cyprus (Acts 13:4-12). As Paul and Barnabas go "through the whole island" (v 6) they encounter "a Jewish false prophet named Bar-Jesus" or "Elymas" (v 6, 8). After the false prophet opposes them, "seeking to turn the proconsul away from the faith" (v 9), Paul goes on to proclaim the following words: "You son of the devil, you enemy of all unrighteousness, full of all deceit and villainy, will you not stop making crooked the straight paths of the Lord?" (v 10). Not stopping there, Paul even blinds the man through "the hand of the Lord" (v 11). This last phrase is interesting because it indicates that the Lord was clearly in approval of such measures, just as in the beginning, before Paul begins his diatribe, we are told he is "filled with the Holy Spirit" (v 9).

Although today's church would call this harsh and ineffective, Barnabas never condemns Paul. When Paul is later

---

[1] Timothy B. Bayly, "Foreword" to *Persecution in the Early Church* (Bloomington, IL: Clearnote Press, 2014), xi.

beaten, stoned, and chased out of cities, something that would offend most Western Christians, the church never turns their back on Paul for being too scandalous or unloving.

We could imagine Paul bringing a resume as outlined in 2 Corinthians 11 to a church in our day. He tells them he has been imprisoned "far more" times than most ministers of the gospel. He has been lashed thirty-nine times on five different occasions and beaten with rods three other times. He has even been stoned once. Most churches would call Paul a trouble-maker and want nothing to do with him, but Paul calls this boasting (2 Cor. 11:16), which implies there is something successful about the above list of achievements. We can assume the Corinthian church that received Paul's letter would agree, otherwise he would have used another line of argument. He was intentionally bringing things up about his background that would verify his authenticity as an Apostle. If Paul had thought the Corinthians would view such turmoil with sneers or critique, he would not have mentioned it. Today it would be different. The modern church would see this as a mark against Paul, not for him. This goes to show how far our churches have veered away from the Apostolic method when it comes to evangelism. Paul would be unwelcomed in most churches today, not only for his lack of eloquence (2 Cor. 11:6), but for being a troubler of the world (Acts 17:6).

Evangelism's Righteous Scandal

In the West today, Christians have the mindset that if we are going to be relevant in the culture, we must keep quiet outside our homes and churches about the gospel, or at the very least, come up with ways and methods that will allow evangelism to be inoffensive. We don't want to be judgmental or intolerant, after all. We don't want our churches to have a bad reputation. Christians today are so fearful of what outsiders think of them that they assume evangelism is best done when it does not arouse hostility, and whenever it does, the person responsible should be disciplined or at least rebuked by the church on account of it. The Christian community considers any kind of scandal or outrage from the unbelieving world to be a mark of woeful ineffectiveness. This was never the case with Paul and the early church:

> Men entering the ministry today seek to imitate the Apostle Paul in giving themselves to church planting, yet our methods bear little resemblance to his. Technique and affect are everything: hipster eyeglass frames, cool web design, androgynous musicians, women up front administering the Sacraments, fellow-traveler sermons.... Whatever, as long as we make sure we never mention the idols on every street corner and we absolutely never call men to repent. We nurture and gather, reassuring our prospects that we don't believe in judging anyone. We blather on about grace, Gospel-centrality, and being 'in the city and for the city.' Naturally, we soon have our flash mob. This is the opposite of the Early Church's Gospel witness.[2]

The early Church never attempted truce or neutrality with those who were perishing. There was a clear, firm call to repent

---

[2] Bayly, "Foreword" to *Persecution in the Early Church*, xii.

and believe the gospel, and they were violently goaded by the world because of it. Their churches had terrible "reviews." The Western church today has become emasculated by comparison. Our fangs are gone. We have become timid and effeminate. Christians who don't fit into such a mold, boldly proclaiming the gospel instead, "are censored, ostracized, mocked, and scorned. Their spouses divorce them and they lose custody of their children. Their job applications are thrown out and their tenure is denied."[3] Tragically, in many cases their brothers and sisters in Christ refuse fellowship with them or refuse to support them in the work of evangelism. When John and Peter were arrested, the church prays for them. When Paul is chased out of cities, the brothers are alongside encouraging him. Even when Paul is abandoned by certain friends, it is never because he is too scandalous, but because the helpers have fallen into worldliness or apathy (2 Tim. 4:10).

The Christian church in the West has forgotten the positive impact of scandal. In attempting to accommodate our evangelism to the culture, we have lost the appeal of being a savor of death to the dying (2 Cor. 2:16). As noisome as such an odor is, it is still going to cause an awareness of the gospel, whether or not it is believed. The early church was successful in part because of their utter disregard of what the culture thought about them, even in the face of persecution. Few Christians evangelize like this today, and sadly, the few who do become persecuted by other Christians as much as they are by the world. One pastor has noticed the same thing: "Usually, those who get the angriest with my trying to talk about Jesus

---

[3] Bayly, "Foreword" to *Persecution in the Early Church*, xiv.

with them are those who have already 'gone to church' that week. They view my conversation with them as inappropriate because it is not being confined to the appropriate place, the church building."[4]

Christians who want to accommodate evangelism to the culture disregard the fact that this was never Christ's approach, nor was it the way of the early Christians. George Whitefield, John Wesley, David Brainerd, and even William Carey were considered a scandal by the church community for their refusal to compromise with current evangelism practices. They were zealots. They were radicals. They were willing to be fools for Christ's sake, and the church was embarrassed by them. Consider John Ryland's response to the criticism of William Carey by other clergymen in their day: "I am almost worn out with grief at these foolish cavils against some of the best of my brethren, men of God, who are only hated because of their zeal."[5] Michael A.G. Haykin notes that one of the hurdles William Carey had to overcome was "the lack of support by fellow Christians in England."[6]

The Apostle Paul, Whitefield, and Luther were reckless at times, yet today they are the darlings of the Reformed church. It is interesting how much George Whitefield is loved among the Reformed community today, for example, but when someone begins to evangelize in the same way Whitefield did, many are quick to criticize it as too boisterous—especially if, like Whitefield, the preacher does not have the church's approval.

---

[4] Joe Kohler, *The Forgotten Officer* (Bloomington, IN: WestBow Press, 2016), 31.

[5] Cited in A. de M. Chesterman, "The Journals of Daniel Brainerd and of William Carey," *The Baptist Quarterly* 19 (1961-62): 151-52.

[6] Michael H.G. Haykin, *The Missionary Fellowship of William Carey* (Sanford, FL: Reformation Trust Publishing, 2018), 5.

(Scott Smith and I have argued elsewhere for the importance of the local church and evangelism.)[7] The moment such evangelism invokes the same hostility and scandal that Whitefield did, many in the church run the other way or shuts it down. Such a phenomenon is marvelously illustrated by Spurgeon:

> Everybody admires Luther! Yes, yes; but you do not want any one else to do the same today. When you go to the Zoological Gardens you all admire the bear; but how would you like a bear at home, or a bear wandering loose about the street?.... So, we admire a man who was firm in the faith, say four hundred years ago; the past ages are a sort of bear-pit or iron cage for him; but such a man today is a nuisance, and must be put down.[8]

Biblical Confrontation

It is one thing for the world to hate the Christian, especially for his bold evangelism. Christ Himself told us we should expect it. But why do Christians themselves condemn it? Why do Christians shy away from confrontation, when in the Scriptures it was never so? R. C. Sproul notes that "Jesus' life was a storm of controversy. The apostles, like the prophets before them, could hardly go a day without controversy. Paul said that he debated daily in the marketplace. To avoid controversy is to avoid Christ."[9] We carefully make sure our worship and

---

[7] See *A Certain Sound: A Primer on Open Air Preaching* (Grand Rapids, MI: Reformation Heritage Press, 2019).

[8] Charles H. Spurgeon, "Holding Fast the Faith," The Metropolitan Tabernacle Pulpit, Vol. 34 (London: Passmore and Alabaster, 1888), 78, 83.

[9] R. C. Sproul, *Essential Truths of the Christian Faith* (Carol Stream, IL: Tyndale House Publishers, 1992), xv.

preaching are biblical but when it comes to our evangelism, anything similar to the models in the Bible is condemned, especially if it brings about the same backlash that we see Paul and Jesus receiving:

> Thus in the Church today, the man who...awakens anger or hostility against our Lord and His people, his brothers in Christ accuse him of not showing Christian humility and compassion. Likely he was dogmatic, his choice of time and place was poor, he sounded political, he tried to force his religion down people's throats, his word choices were calculated to inflame postmodern sensibilities; or, worst of all, he quoted the Bible.[10]

How can we account for this? Were the ways of the early church too reckless or harsh? Would we be right to criticize Paul for the times he was stoned, whipped, or beaten, since we criticize such confrontational Christians in our own day? In general, the church has unwittingly bought into the idea that peace at all costs is the best way to evangelize. The church seems to think that if the culture or individuals are upset when the Christian evangelizes, the reproach to Christianity won't gain converts and we should try another method. But reproach and scoffing are exactly the responses we should expect when it comes to biblical evangelism, as are arrests and confiscation of property. In fact, why would we assume any other response? The world's eyes are veiled to the gospel (2 Cor. 4:3). There are none who seek God (Rom. 3:11). But a church culture that sees salvific success as the most important aim of evangelism, hence

---

[10] Bayly, "Foreword" to *Persecution in the Early Church*, xi.

"even if one," will also claim that any approach that brings conflict or polarization must necessarily be jettisoned—especially if there is no "one" who is saved.

The idea that any kind of hostility against Christians is a bad thing for the church—even if induced by bold evangelism—has betrayed the church's misunderstanding of what happens when the gospel is faithfully proclaimed to the lost. In a hardened atmosphere like the contemporary West, hatred from the world will typically happen far more often than the conversion of "the one." While the church welcomes the conversion of the one, it does not welcome the hatred of the world.

College Ministries in the West

One of the best examples of this is what happens with college ministries. Colleges and universities are some of the darkest mission fields in the Western world. Naturalism, sexual immorality, abortion and homosexual rights are all part of the curriculum, whether officially or unofficially. The age of most college students places them in a very formative time of life. Christians have rightly acknowledged the need for regular gospel witness in such atmospheres. Evangelicals from all denominations attempt to bring some form of the gospel to the students. What you will also find upon closer examination is that most campus ministries are approaching this mission field through unbiblical methodologies. An attempt to not offend the students seems to be the chief desire. Rather than coming forth and boldly, even openly placing the gospel onto the lampstand of the campus, "so that those who come in may see the light," many seem to cover it under the lid of social projects and ultimate frisbee in fear that the actual gospel may anger or provoke students to dissociate themselves with the campus ministry.

As a case example, one year before ministering at an Ivy League school, our evangelism team reached out to the director of the Reformed ministry on that particular campus. The email read as follows:

> We are Reformed ministers who'll be coming with a team of evangelists this fall to the —- campus. We are looking for likeminded campus ministries to join hands with for the sake of having some local people to disciple students. Like Jesus and the Apostles, we go, stand, and preach the gospel of Christ. Let me know if you're interested.

A few days later we received a response from the campus minister: "We hope for fruit in your endeavors, but I believe we have to decline the offer on methodological grounds." This was the entirety of the minister's email. What is unusual about the response is his reason for not joining. We sent a follow up email to seek clarification on what he meant by "methodological grounds." We never received a response.

This is a bigger issue than a team of evangelists feeling jaded by a campus minister. What is at stake is the gospel and the way we go about sharing it with the lost. We would expect such a view of evangelism from an Arminian who believes it possible to "push someone further away" or thinks it necessary to make the gospel as "attractive" as possible to an unbeliever for the sake of enticing his "free" will, but not from a Reformed minister. In this case the problem cannot be theological, since we assumingly hold to the same doctrinal truths, unless there is an inconsistency somewhere when it comes to evangelism. An alternative reason may be that he fears losing esteem or reputation in the eyes of the students. He may fear that a bad reputation among lost college students will hurt the ministry's presence on campus. He likely fears suffering or becoming a reproach for the sake of the gospel. Even if he felt uncomfortable preaching Christ himself, what would keep him from coming alongside to share the gospel or follow up with the interested students? Although he said it is due to methodological reasons, what else can be put forward other than fear of persecution or an inconsistency in his supposed Reformed convictions?

Most campus ministries are woefully ashamed of making any kind of fuss on the campus, and the gospel has been shuttered because of it. Campus ministries try to behave as clownish and saccharine as possible, thinking it will attract unbelieving students who are also clownish and saccharine.

The Curse of Affluence

It should also be noted that Christians in the West, because of affluence, have become soft. To an extent we cannot help this. Most of us were born into such an environment. It is impossible to remove ourselves from the influences in which we have been brought up. But it still does not negate its truthfulness. We are soft. We don't like confrontation. We don't like discomfort, whether physically or emotionally.

Perhaps this is why the modern church emphasizes being winsome when evangelizing. According to Webster's Dictionary, the definition for winsome is "generally pleasing and

engaging often because of a childlike charm and innocence."
The second definition is "cheerful, lighthearted." When tagged
onto evangelism, such definitions should help show how far
winsome is from the biblical method. This is not to say that
we should be harsh or calloused in our approach to the lost.
We should strive for tenderness and unfeigned compassion.
But the words "bold" and "somber" are used as descriptions
for biblical evangelism (Acts 4:13, 29; 14:3; Eph. 6:19-20; 1
Thess. 1:5; 2:2), never "pleasing" or charming.

The word winsome is likely an unintentional way to justify
being diffident and unprovocative when sharing the gospel.
It justifies the Christian who wants to temper any unpleasant or negative responses when evangelizing. But neither the
early church nor the Scriptures knew of any such phrase as
"winsome." It would seem that Paul, the early disciples, and
the Old Testament prophets would have seen such a phrase as
"winsome" as a means of self-preservation when it comes to
sharing the gospel. On the contrary, Will Metzger describes
the liberation of being bold when evangelizing: "The doxo-
logical (worshipping) evangelist, therefore, is bold and not
as concerned about the opinions of others. Delivered from
worrying about others' opinions, they act for an audience of
One."[11] The "one" that we should be concerned about is the
Lord, not the lost, as much as we desire the lost to be saved
and as much as we should behave in a compassionate, God-
honoring way.

Christians today have a tendency to tell the person who
evangelizes boldly that he is "not loving enough" or he is "too

---

[11] Will Metzger, *Tell the Truth* (Downers Grove, IL: InterVarsity, 1981), 183.

judgmental." They will say he is pushing sinners "further" away. In most scenarios the problem comes from the professing Christian not knowing or not believing his Bible as it relates to evangelism. These kinds of Christians will see the response of the unregenerate world. They will hear the scoffing. Then they will conclude that brash evangelism must therefore be "wrong." They will say it is harmful. But the Christian must stick to the Bible for his justification to share Christ boldly. The Scriptures show that this kind of response is expected from those dead in sin, as well as from professing Christians who have not submitted to God's word in this area.

It does not mean the Christian should intentionally antagonize or look for such a response while evangelizing. It does not mean the Christian should dismiss advice or correction when it comes to evangelism, especially when it is coming from his local church. The Christian should never intentionally try to look foolish or provoke people's ire. He should not try to prove himself by seeing how many people want to kill him. But anyone faithfully proclaiming the Word of God will encounter a stiff-necked and adulterous generation and the typical responses generated because of it.

The Early Church: Brash Evangelism, Not Peace at All Costs

Brash evangelism led to both converts and persecution in the early church, but it was still the talk of society. Today the church has a backwards view. We believe that less conflict will produce more salvific results. We believe that the more Christianity can fit in and be liked by culture, the more it will attract a lost world and hopefully "the one" will be saved because of it. But this is exactly where we go wrong, as demonstrated by what happened in the early church:

> The conflict was inevitable, the direct result of the genius of Christianity. A Christianity which had ceased to be aggressive would speedily have ceased to exist. Christ came not to send peace on earth but a sword; against the restless and resistless force of the new religion the gates of hell should not prevail. But polytheism could not be dethroned without a struggle; nor mankind regenerated without a baptism of blood. Persecution, in fact, is the other side of aggression, the inevitable outcome of a truly missionary spirit; the two are linked together as action and reaction.[12]

Part of the attraction of Christianity in its infancy was its bold, uncompromising gospel proclamation. It hurled the gospel directly into the teeth of the fiercest, most ruthless society ever known to man, and despite the persecutions such action inevitably brought upon them, they dug in and preached even harder. That is attractive in the biblical sense. That is supernatural. Unlike the early church, today's "evangelicalism has lost its tolerance for confrontative preaching."[13] The early Christians were considered aggressive and imprudent by the surrounding culture, even while other religions were taking steps to avoid persecution. Oddly enough, such boldness was what attracted the surrounding culture to consider Christian-

---

[12] Herbert B. Workman, *Persecution in the Early Church* (Bloomington, IL: Clearnote Press, 2014), 39.

[13] John MacArthur, *Ashamed of the Gospel* (Wheaton, IL: Crossway Books, 1993), 50.

ity more closely: "The mysteries of the Christians, on the other hand, were the secrets of men who would not stoop to secure either official sanction or popular support, but who yet, by the very necessities of their religion and its mission, were aggressive, perhaps at times imprudent, enthusiasts."[14]

Compare it with the church today. We know that such an approach to evangelism will cause hatred from the world, but rather than do it anyways, we retreat into a corner, put the gospel away, and hand out water bottles with encouraging one-liner Bible verses, smiling and saying, "God loves you." We offer to build houses or have carnivals for the lost. We refuse to do anything that would cause a gospel scandal. What drives such soft-peddled approaches to evangelism except a fear of man and a disbelief in the power of the gospel to save?

One could even argue that such approaches to evangelism are syncretistic and idolatrous. It is an attempt to assimilate the culture into the gospel message, or willing to compromise in a tolerant and even relativistic way. We make ourselves part of whatever cultural fad is in vogue for the sake of "being all things to all people," which is really just shaving down the gospel so that persecution is kept far away. On the other hand, rather than trying to blend in with their culture, the early church "emblazoned on its banners its loathing and disdain for the cults."[15] It never sought "friendship with the world" (James 4:4). It did not "love the world or the things in the world" (1 John 2:15). Naturally this led Christians to the lions or to the stake, but in doing so, paradoxically, it also conquered the

---

[14] Workman, *Persecution in the Early Church*, 122

[15] Workman, *Persecution in the Early Church*, 65.

world, since the world began to take notice of such boldness. The unbelievers realized this was something different.

Today we shrink from the world's hatred and so preach a different gospel. We try to be winsome and lighthearted since our culture is that way. In doing so the world, always smarter than we assume, sees through the sham and recognizes our fear of suffering and fear of man. What is worse, they see our disbelief in the gospel. Such a compromised approach would never have conquered the world in the time of the early church, and neither will it do so today.

The Reformed church has fallen into this trap as well. Rather than establish a better, more biblical method of evangelism founded on the gospel and intercessory prayer, we have embraced the mindset that if the culture is upset with our evangelism method, the fault must be the one sharing the gospel, not the culture. We have forgotten that the gospel "is disturbing, revolting, upsetting, confrontive, convicting, and offensive to human pride."[16] If the world criticizes us for being too judgmental or too brash, we believe it imperils our chance to be a "good witness" for Christ. These views are not Reformed. They are Arminian. Yet Reformed groups have unwittingly adopted them. Presbyterian evangelist Al Baker notices the same thing:

> We are simply not getting the job done on reaching the lost with the gospel. If you read the leading pastors today you will find that most no longer believe you can lead someone to Christ in a one time, spiritual conversation, that street preaching, door to door, or survey evangelism does not

---

[16] MacArthur, *Ashamed of the Gospel*, 84.

work. They say that we live in a different era, in a post-modern world where people no longer believe in heaven or hell.[17]

The cross will always appear foolish to those who are perishing because it attacks people at their pride, whether it is intellectual, physical, monetary, or spiritual. This is also why we have a natural tendency to shrink from conflict and to condemn anyone who brings conflict upon the church when evangelizing. The church must never forget it is through the foolishness of preaching, not catering to man's will, that dead men come alive. Softening the cross with clever speech or eloquence can only create false converts who are drawn to the cleverness or eloquence rather than Christ (1 Cor. 2:1-2). Trying to meet the unbeliever on "neutral ground" or "where he's at" can only lead to the hardening of the unbeliever, which justifies his rebellion against God.

God has always used humble means to save dead souls, not eloquence or pomp, because in doing so God gets all the glory (1 Cor. 2:4-5). And when the Christian is criticized by the world, the only place he will be understood and prayed for is in the church. Let us make it a point to not condemn bold evangelism or those who engage in it, but rather to encourage it and to be about it ourselves. Let us come down from our ivory studies, helpful as they are, and bring what we have learned to the lost. The days of soft-peddled methodologies must end. The days of Arminian approaches to evangelism must end. These are the days when the churches in the West must train Christians to

---

[17] Al Baker, "What the Civil Magistrate Can and Cannot Do," *Forget None of His Benefits Newsletter*, Vol. 17, Number 44 (Nov 8, 2018).

preach Christ in the teeth of persecution and death. We must seek to turn the world upside down with the gospel. We must stir things up, not obnoxiously, but boldly and without shame of the scandal that the gospel causes. Louis Berkhof provides a rousing call to arms in his *Systematic Theology*, with which we end the chapter:

> The Church…is duty bound to carry on an incessant warfare against the hostile world in every form in which it reveals itself, whether in the Church or outside of it, and against all spiritual forces of darkness. The Church may not spend all her time in prayer and meditation, however necessary and important these may be, nor may she rest on her oars in the peaceful enjoyment of her spiritual heritage. She must be engaged with all her might in the battles of her Lord, fighting in a war that is both offensive and defensive.[18]

---

[18] Louis Berkhof, *Systematic Theology* (Carlisle, PA: The Banner of Truth, 1958), 565.

CHAPTER 7

Failed Evangelism

FAILED EVANGELISM is when a person compromises or discounts what the Bible says about evangelism and replaces it with something more "effective." Failed evangelism may see many "converts." It may see a lot of church growth. It may produce speaking engagements every night of the year. It may see swelling crowds when preaching in the open air. But how did it happen? Was God's Word meddled with or made secondary, knowing that otherwise it would not have seen as much numerical success? Were certain parts of the gospel toned down, say on hell or judgment or counting the cost, in order to protect the reputation of the messenger, or worse, the gospel? "External criteria such as affluence, numbers, money, or positive response have never been the biblical measure of success in ministry.... Real success is doing the will of God regardless of the consequences."[1]

Any approach to evangelism that makes something other than gospel proclamation the primary instrument is unbiblical and hence a failure. This would include most types of "friendship evangelism," creative evangelism, seeker-sensitive evangelism, or any other pragmatic attempt to tone down or make secondary the affront of the cross.[2] These methods, though prevalent in our day, are by no means unique. Spurgeon addresses similar trends in the 1800s: "This practice suggests that we are supposed to conceal truth and utter a half-falsehood in order to save souls...This is to suggest that we are to coax sinners into faith by exaggerating one part of the truth and hiding the rest until a more convenient time."[3] Even Augustine comments on such a trend in the fifth century: "What is blameworthy is, that they who themselves revolt from the conduct of the wicked, and live in quite another fashion, yet spare those faults in other men... because they fear to give offense."[4] Later he comments: "Nor is that man guiltless of the sin we speak of, who, though he be not a watchman, yet sees in the conduct of those with whom the relationships of this life bring into contact, many things that should be blamed, and yet overlooks them, fearing to give offence and

---

[1] John MacArthur, *Ashamed of the Gospel* (Wheaton, IL: Crossway Books, 1993), 42.

[2] Sharing the gospel with friends is different from the "friendship evangelism" method, which intentionally deceives a person into friendship for the sake of sprinkling in the gospel at a more convenient time. It assumes that a friendship is necessary for a person to "receive" the gospel in a salvific way.

[3] Charles H. Spurgeon, *The Soul Winner* (Abbotsford, WI: Life Sentence Publishing, 2016), 8.

[4] Augustine, *City of God*, Tr. Marcus Dods (New York: Random House, 1993), 13.

lose such worldly blessings as may legitimately be desired, but which he too eagerly grasps."[5]

Spurgeon notes that such pragmatic measures are done "because it is supposed that no conversions will occur if he preaches the whole counsel of God."[6] Spurgeon also has a strong opinion about the devastation of such compromise: "The withholding of the doctrine of the total depravity of man has brought about serious harm to many who have listened to such preaching. The people don't experience a true healing, because they don't recognize the disease under which they suffer."[7] Anyone who attempts to evangelize with such a gospel is a failure, regardless of the numerical results that come from it.

On the other hand, the Christian who faithfully shares the gospel from a motive of love for God and love for man can never be a failure when evangelizing. He may never see anyone saved. He may never receive an invitation to speak at a conference. He may never see a crowd when preaching in the open air. He may never have any statistics to boast of in his newsletter or denomination report. His church may not grow. But if he is faithful to the biblical prescription for evangelism, he is successful. This is not to say we should be satisfied with empty nets, but it is to say that the mark of "successful" evangelism should never be the number of conversions or how many people rush to the messenger or his church. This is why Paul was successful despite failing in the eyes of the world:

---

[5] Augustine, *City of God*, 13.
[6] Spurgeon, *The Soul Winner*, 8.
[7] Spurgeon, *The Soul Winner*, 9.

Externally, it may have seemed to the world that Paul was a failure. He was arrested, imprisoned for years, and finally killed by the Roman officials. Yet even in those dark hours Paul kept preaching. When he couldn't preach to crowds, he preached to the soldiers assigned to guard him. When he couldn't minister in the churches, he ministered in the prisons. He was always ready to preach—but never to compromise.[8]

The fact that he was stoned and left for dead (Acts 14:19), beaten, imprisoned, and finally killed for the truth's sake ought to demonstrate that he didn't adapt the message to make it pleasing to his hearers! And the personal suffering he bore because of his ministry did not indicate that something was wrong with his approach, but that everything had been right![9]

This is why successful evangelism is being faithful to the mandates of the Bible, regardless of the effect that such a mandate produces.

The Chief End is Not Man

The Christian who regularly shares the gospel will be asked how many people he has led to Christ. His answer should be, "all of them," since every time he shares the gospel, people are led to Christ. If they have been told the gospel, including the mandate to believe it, they have been led to the cross. What happens next is up to the Lord. This is why the gospel is always one-hundred percent "effective." There is always a one-hundred percent "response" rate. Some have ears to hear.

---

[8] MacArthur, *Ashamed of the Gospel*, 139.
[9] MacArthur, *Ashamed of the Gospel*, 103.

Some gnash their teeth. Some walk past silently. Some leap and rejoice at the preaching of the gospel. But everyone responds. The gospel is never neutral. The gospel is never ineffective. As Spurgeon notes,

> To endeavor to save men by absurd or nonsensical talk, ideas, excitement, or rhetorical display is as foolish as to hope to hold an angel with adhesive or to lure a star with music. The best attraction is the gospel in its purity. The weapon with which the Lord conquers men is the truth as it is in Jesus. The gospel has the same magnitude in every emergency – an arrow which can pierce the hardest heart, and a balm which will heal the deadliest wound. Preach it, and preach nothing else. Rely implicitly upon the old, old gospel. You need no other nets when you fish for men. Those your Master has given you are strong enough for the great fish and have mesh fine enough to hold the little ones. Spread these nets and no others, and you'll have no need to fear the fulfilment of His Word. I will make you fishers of men (Matt. 4:19).[10]

Modern evangelism has made man the chief end of all their efforts. Modern evangelism has made the "method" the chief means of saving the lost. This is not exactly wrong. We should have a method when evangelizing. But when looking to Scripture, as we have seen, the only methods we are given are intercessory prayer and the gospel. When it comes to evangelism, we must put aside our obsession for results. We must shatter our idolatry of reputation. We must go forth for the purpose of

---

[10] Spurgeon, *The Soul Winner*, 8.

glorifying God and obeying Him in the work He has called us to do, which is to share Christ, even if none are saved. Calvin said the same thing in the sixteenth century:

> Whatever may be the issue of our preaching, it is, notwith-standing, well-pleasing to God, if the gospel is preached... it does not detract in any degree from the dignity of the gospel that it does not do good to all; for God is glorified even in this, that the gospel becomes an occasion of ruin to the wicked, nay, it must turn out so.[11]

Most Western Christians believe if someone is repelled by the gospel message it is the fault of the message or messenger, not the person offended. They are surprised to learn that gospel proclamation often leads to persecution and rejection. They are surprised that even if none are saved or respond "favorably" to the message, it is still worth sharing, and the person sharing it is not a failure. Perhaps they would be appalled to learn that most of the time in our culture, not just occasionally, God does not save anyone when the gospel is shared, nor is God required to. In fact, when the gospel is proclaimed outside church walls, most people are greatly offended, whether or not they show it. This does not mean we should try something else or deem our efforts fruitless.

Even in Reformed circles, the approach to evangelism and ministry in general is overly concerned with results, especially as it relates to reputation. Many churches are not bothered by staying stagnant in matters of evangelism, so long as other Reformed groups know they are solid in their teaching. This

---

[11] John Calvin, tr. John Pringle, *Commentary on the Epistles of Paul the Apostle to the Corinthians*, (2015), 417.

is different from the obsession for numbers and results, but it amounts to the same thing: the lost are being cheated, and the Great Commission is being neglected. Desiring a reputation for doctrinal success can become idolatrous and disadvantageous to our duty to evangelize. Obsession for reputation can lead us to be concerned with being hip, cool, sound, or calculatingly intelligent, even though it is completely at odds with the messy, uncouth, and confrontational approach of Paul. As important as doctrinal soundness is, it is not an excuse for refusing to turn the world upside down with the gospel (Acts 17:6). "Men like Elijah, Elisha, Isaiah, and Ezekiel persevered in the midst of rejection, persecution, and affliction because they were far more concerned with being faithful than with being popular. In their own day, they were viewed as eccentric outcasts and failures. But from heaven's perspective, they epitomize true success."[12]

Have People Changed?

One of the chief arguments against biblical evangelism is that people have changed over the course of two thousand years, and we should therefore use a different approach. We are told that the world does not respond well to preaching, so we should adjust our method accordingly. But aside from the fact that the world has never responded well to biblical preaching, which is demonstrated by the constant afflictions of Paul and even Jesus, this argument is made from an anthropocentric perspective. It looks at the results of biblical

---

[12] Nathan Busenitz, "The Word of Truth in a World of Error," *Evangelism* (Nashville, TN: Thomas Nelson, 2011), 58.

preaching and assumes that the one evangelizing is sovereign over a person's conversion, not God. It assumes man's wisdom can determine which times and seasons will be most successful with the gospel, as opposed to acknowledging it is God's prerogative alone to bring a harvest. It assumes man knows best about what our fellow human beings need spiritually, rather than submitting to God's methods. But biblical evangelism must not change because of the responses from the culture:

> That is what we mean by "biblical evangelism." Its success is not measured by immediate numeric results. It does not have to be retooled or completely redesigned if at first glance it does not seem to be working. It stays focused on the cross and the message of redemption, undiluted by pragmatic or worldly interests. It is never obsessed with questions like how people might react, what we can do to make our message more appealing, or how we might frame the gospel differently so as to minimize the offense of the cross. It is concerned instead with truth, clarity, biblical accuracy, and (above all) Christ.[13]

John Owen reminds us that the cause of salvation is the sovereign will and pleasure of God, and thus "the times and seasons of the prevalency of the gospel in the world are in the hand and at the sovereign disposal of God."[14] Owen points out that God "is not obliged...to accompany it (the gospel) with

---

[13] John MacArthur and Jesse Johnson, "Rediscovering Biblical Evangelism," *Evangelism* (Nashville, TN: Thomas Nelson, 2011), ix.

[14] John Owen, *The Work of the Spirit* (Carlisle, PA: The Banner of Truth Trust: 1967), 43.

the same power at all times and seasons."[15] The *Second London Baptist Confession* says the same thing in chapter 20:3:

> The revelation of the gospel unto sinners, made in divers times and by sundry parts, with the addition of promises and precepts for the obedience required therein, as to the nations and persons to whom it is granted, is merely of the sovereign will and good pleasure of God; not being annexed by virtue of any promise to the due improvement of men's natural abilities, by virtue of common light received without it, which none ever did make, or can do so; and therefore in all ages, the preaching of the gospel has been granted unto persons and nations, as to the extent or straitening of it, in great variety, according to the counsel of the will of God.

Rather than change the God-given methods of gospel proclamation and prayer, we should recognize that God is under no obligation to save any soul and to praise Him all the more for the people who have been saved. Rather than assume our evangelism has failed, we should be all the more eager to be about the Master's business, knowing His sheep will hear His voice, and that they do so through the timeless method of gospel proclamation and prayer.

The Offense of Evangelism

Biblical evangelism can never be done in an "unconfrontational" manner. The very nature of evangelism is, in a sense, confrontational. It is getting into people's spiritual spaces. It

---

[15] Owen, *The Work of the Spirit*, 43.

cannot be done otherwise. This is not to dismiss discernment and propriety when it comes to sharing the gospel. This is not to say we should be disrespectful about it. But evangelism is openly acknowledging that the person you are witnessing to is wrong about what they believe and live for, and if they continue down such a road, they will die in their sins and be condemned to hell. This is naturally confrontational, whether or not it leads to actual confrontation. The only way to get around it is by compromising the gospel, which is exactly what many Christians have done when it comes to evangelism. Others simply stop evangelizing altogether.

This is why the desire to make "confrontational evangelism" only one of several methods of evangelism is misleading. It gives the impression that confrontational evangelism is more aggressive and mean-spirited than the more relational types. But in reality even the softer, more relational types of evangelism must be confrontational, otherwise they fail to be categorized as biblical: "Relational evangelism, in spite of its good intentions, often does not emphasize hearing the word of truth as necessary kindling that the Holy Spirit ignites in regeneration (Rom. 10:17). Relational evangelism's approach can neglect the theological content of the gospel by shifting the focus to the personality and experience of the evangelist."[16]

In another place Metzger points out that "what may have begun as an attempt to relate to nonbelievers by being more loving, relational and personal, ends up putting the person at the center, not God. Where is our confidence in the unique inspiration and divine authority of God's written Word?"[17]

---

[16] Will Metzger, *Tell the Truth* (Downers Grove, IL: InterVarsity, 1981), 211.

[17] Metzger, *Tell the Truth*, 17.

Earlier in the book he warns, "Is your evangelism only relational? Take heed."[18]

When one realizes the gospel includes the realities of repentance, hell, and counting the cost, and that a lost man will likely be offended when you share this with him, it becomes apparent why holding back such truths would be pleasant to the flesh. People get upset when such topics are applied to them. We naturally do not like it when people are upset with us: "The greatest obstacle in personal evangelism is fear...We fear what others will think of us, that they might reject us. Proverbs tells us fear of man is a trap; it immobilizes us."[19] Ernest C. Reisinger agrees that our fear of man causes us to leave such hard doctrines out: "Now, this message of repentance almost got Paul killed...And one of the reasons preachers avoid preaching repentance is this very point. It will cause some waves and some antagonism from this generation of poor, lost, self-deceived church members who are products of an evangelism that has left repentance out of its message."[20]

Biblical evangelism should not expect any applause or appreciation from the people. It should not expect any "favorable" results in a worldly sense, and when we do see an interest in Christ, we should be patient and cautious, examining to see if it is of God or man. What Michael Green says regarding the response to the early church's evangelism should be applied to any age, including our own: "They could not do less than go and preach the gospel to all who would hear. And once preached it could not but be divisive because it would not fit

---

[18] Metzger, *Tell the Truth*, 77.

[19] Metzger, *Tell the Truth*, 145.

[20] Ernest C. Reisinger, *Today's Evangelism* (Philipsburg, NJ: Craig Press, 1982), 30.

in with the comfortable contemporary synthesis of religions, but made absolute claims on a person's loyalty and allegiance in the name of an absolute God."[21]

It is easy to take a lost person to supper or have them over to the house for a barbecue. There will be no offense or scandal in doing so. It is easy to bring lost people to a church filled with fog machines and carnal music and preaching that only deals with social woes. It is easy to show a lost person the love of Jesus without ever communicating the exclusivity of His claims. Many modern Christians hide behind these flesh-driven methods, assuming they are being obedient to Christ for doing so. Their chief desire is to look palatable in the eyes of sinners. Driven by fear of rejection, they tone down the demands of the cross, and so preach a different gospel altogether. But such fear is not worthy of our Lord Jesus Christ, and it does not appreciate enough that rejection and "negative reactions" are often good signs that the gospel is pricking the conscience:

> Sometimes we find ourselves put off by what we deem to be a negative reaction, forgetting that when the gospel comes, it often does bite unbelievers' consciences, and they kick—sometimes hard—against the goads before finally they submit to the righteousness of God. That anger, bitterness, aggression, or some other spiritual venom may be an initial response to the truth pressed home by the Spirit of God in someone's heart. Therefore, press on.[22]

---

[21] Michael Green, *Evangelism in the Early Church* (Grand Rapids, MI: W. B. Eerdmans, 1970), 220.

[22] Jeremy Walker, *The Brokenhearted Evangelist* (Grand Rapids, MI: Reformation Heritage Books, 2012), 76.

The Christian who presents the beauty of Christ to the world will discover most are blind and unwilling to look upon Him. The seed will often fall on hard ground (Matt 13:1-23). The professing Christian who is unfamiliar with biblical evangelism will see such rejection as harmful or useless. But rejection corroborates perfectly with what God's Word says regarding evangelism: "The natural man does not receive the things of the Spirit of God, for they are foolishness to him; nor can he know them, because they are spiritually discerned" (1 Cor. 2:14). Or again, "Our gospel is veiled...to those who are perishing, whose minds the god of this age has blinded, who do not believe, lest the light of the gospel of the glory of Christ, who is the image of God, should shine on them" (2 Cor. 4:3-4). Such responses are not an indication of failed evangelism. They are a reminder that God's Word is true, and such a response to the gospel has been taking place for more than 2,000 years.

The early church provides us with another example of brash, unashamed evangelism in the face of a hostile culture. They too lived in a world where religious tolerance was the most important value in society. They lived in an age when exclusivist claims regarding religion was politically incorrect and even illegal. But the Christians of that era made it their business to openly oppose all forms of idolatry. How else can you account for the persecution that came against them from all the world? How else can you account for the fact that both pagans and Jews attempted to violently expunge them?

When it comes to the West's attitude today towards uncompromising Christianity, it is the same we see in the early church: "The Roman Empire found it intolerable two millennia ago, and we've come full circle. Once again Christian witness has become divisive and the American Empire finds it intolerable."[23] This is why today "true Christian witness that condemns idolatry and warns of God's judgment is condemned as 'inflammatory rhetoric' or 'hate speech' and must be silenced."[24] And how do many Western Christians respond? There are only two options. We can we stop boldly sharing the gospel and condemn those who continue to do it, seeing the reaction it causes, or we can set our face like flint and hurl ourselves into the maelstrom of persecution. One is a failure, even if the world and modern Christians love him. The other is successful, even if none are saved or he loses his life on account of it.

The goal of the early church was to share the message of Jesus Christ in an uncompromising manner, whether or not it led to someone's salvation: "They were very bold about it, despite the opposition they encountered. There was no trace of compromise in their preaching. They looked for nothing less than total surrender to the Lord and Savior Jesus Christ. Indeed they went out of their way to ridicule pagan gods."[25] It was not the desire to see tangible "success" that induced them to share the gospel, especially in so brash a manner as many of them did. Rather it came as the natural overflow of their worship of Christ. It was urgent, and their belief in its truth kept them from softening it for the sake of a more "positive" response. They would have shared the gospel even had no one

---

[23] Timothy B. Bayly, "Foreword" to *Persecution in the Early Church* (Bloomington, IL: Clearnote Press, 2014), x.

[24] Bayly, "Foreword" to *Persecution in the Early Church*, x.

[25] Michael Green, *Evangelism in the Early Church* (Grand Rapids, MI: Wm. B Eerdmans Publishing Company, 1970), 21.

been saved. They would have seen faithfulness as the mark of "success," even if it led to their death, as it often did.

All Things to All People?

Paul's comment on being "all things to all people" has been abused since the church's beginning (1 Cor. 9-19-23). Tertullian, for instance, talks about Christians in his own day using the verse to justify attendance at heathen rituals or idolatry when with idolaters or adultery when with adulterers. He responds to such hyper-contextualization by saying, "Of course he (God) does not so slacken those reigns of conversations that, since it is necessary for us both to live and mingle with sinners, we may be able to sin with them too."[26] Calvin was also aware of people abusing Paul's words. Speaking on this phrase, he writes: "Those who do not distinguish between things which are neutral, and things which are forbidden, are doubly in the wrong. Because they do not make that distinction they have no hesitation about undertaking things, which God has forbidden, in order to please men. But their crowning sin is their making wrong use of this sentence of Paul's, in order to make excuses for their own wicked hypocrisy."[27]

The popular word today when it comes to evangelism is contextualization. The favorite passage to illustrate contextualization is 1 Corinthians 9. If by contextualization one means preaching in Spanish when in Mexico or not offending cultural norms in the Middle East or on a Navajo Reservation

---

[26] Tertullian, "On Idolatry," *The Ante-Nicene Fathers*, Ed. Alexander Roberts and James Donaldson (Peabody, MA: Hendrickson, 1994), 69.

[27] John Calvin, *The First Epistle of Paul to the Corinthians*, trans. John W. Fraser (Grand Rapids, MIC: Eerdmans, 1960), 196,

in Arizona, then it would be consistent with what Paul has in mind. But "contextualization" does not usually mean this whenever it is used in contemporary conversations about evangelism. Writing about the "contextualization" of the gospel today, John MacArthur says it "has infected the church with the spirit of the age. It has opened the door's wide for worldliness, shallowness, and in some cases a crass, party atmosphere. The world now sets the agenda for the church."[28] This is not just a problem in Arminian camps, either. Reformed camps are now embracing such approaches to evangelism, often without realizing it:

> The perceived mandate is that, if the gospel is to remain relevant, Christianity must somehow adapt and appeal to the latest cultural trends. That kind of thinking used to be limited to the seeker-sensitive crowd, but it has recently made the leap into more Reformed circles. There are entire movements that would agree to the truths of predestination, election, and total depravity, but then also, inexplicably, demand that pastors act more like rock stars than humble shepherds.[29]

It would not be a strawman to describe hyper-contextualization as allowing the world to set the agenda for how we evangelize. Since the world likes amusement, we should include amusement in our evangelism. If we are evangelizing at a college campus, we should try to entice them with college-age activities like foosball, video games, or an occasional beer. If we are evangelizing a group of bikers, we should wear

---

[28] MacArthur, *Ashamed of the Gospel*, 113.
[29] John MacArthur, "Theology of Sleep," *Evangelism* (Nashville, TN: Thomas Nelson, 2011), 10.

a biker's vest and use biker lingo. Better yet, we should buy a Harley Davidson. Making ourselves and the message more attractive to unbelievers will in turn draw them to believe the gospel. The world is attracted to ballets, especially in cosmopolitan New York City, so we should have ballets during our worship services. The world likes skits and humor, so we should use them to break the ice before sharing the gospel with the lost. Spurgeon was not silent about his discontent with such approaches: "If I, or you, or any of us, or all of us, shall have spent our lives merely in amusing men, or educating men, or moralizing men, when we shall come to give our account at the last great day we shall be in a very sorry condition, and we shall have but made a very sorry record to render."[30]

But what did Paul mean by this passage if it wasn't "act like the world so the world will be more attracted to the gospel"? Paul is calling for something opposite of hyper-contextualization. He is calling for "self-denial and sacrifice for those who do not know Christ."[31] Paul claims his motive is "that I might win more of them" (1 Cor. 9:19). Paul is a soul winner. But Paul points out he has deliberately denied himself certain liberties in order to be a more effective soul winner. He has made no use of the rights he has as a preacher of the gospel (v 15). He calls himself "a servant to all." In order "to win Jews" and "that I might win those under the law," he "became as a Jew" and "became as one under the law (though not being myself under the law)" (v 20). In order to "win those outside the law," he "became as one outside the law (not being outside the law

---

[30] Charles H. Spurgeon, "Soul Saving Our One Business," *The Metropolitan Tabernacle Pulpit*, Vol. 25 (London: Passmore & Alabaster, 1879), 674-676.

[31] MacArthur, *Ashamed of the Gospel*, 107.

of God but under the law of Christ)" (v 21). In order to "win the weak," Paul "became weak" (v 22). In order that he "might save some," Paul became "all things to all people" (v 22).

This is a passage about running and winning in matters of evangelism (vv 24-26). It is about being a qualified evangelist who is used by God to bring the gospel to the lost. It is about having an aim and rules when sharing the gospel. It is not about acting like the world in order to attract the world to the gospel. It is not about hiding the gospel behind entertainment and humor or establishing common ground with the hearers. "Current church growth methodology claims that if an evangelist wants to 'reach the culture' (whatever that means), he must emulate the culture in some way. But such an approach runs contrary to the biblical paradigm."[32]

Paul's meaning here is actually incredibly simple: don't offend people unnecessarily. William Carey provides a good illustration of this. One of the agreements that Carey and his colleagues came up with while serving as missionaries in India was to avoid offending non-Christians by their mannerisms: "Those parts of English manners which are most offensive to them (the Indians) should be kept out of sight as much as possible."[33] It does not mean he is going to indulge in cultural extravagances for the sake of making the gospel more attractive to the world, whether it be meat offered to idols or a game of beer pong at a college party. Far from acting like the world for the sake of attracting them to the gospel, Paul is speaking about giving up certain liberties that might be offensive.

---

[32] MacArthur, "Theology of Sleep," *Evangelism*, 3.

[33] "The Serampore Form of Agreement (1805)," Wholesome Words Home, accessed February 21, 2019, www.wholesomewords.org/missions/bcarey13.html.

Peter had the same view when writing to the church in Pontus, Galatia, Cappadocia, Asia, and Bithynia, reminding them to "conduct yourselves in fear during the time of your stay on earth" and that they had been called "out of darkness into his marvelous light" for the purpose of proclaiming "the excellencies of him" (1 Pet. 2:9). Peter reminds them a couple verses later that they are "sojourners and exiles" in the world, and that rather than conforming to the patterns of those around them, they are to stand out as people who are holy. This is exactly the opposite of most modern evangelism approaches:

> Some believe that being familiar with popular culture will make it easier to have conversations with worldly people, but what is the value in discussing what celebrities are dating whom or what sports teams are competing for some title? Do we think we will spend any time in heaven discussing such trivialities? Do we not realize that clothing ourselves in the garb of a futile world culture is a walk in futility?[34]

Later on it is noted,

> Those who teach that Christians should blend in with the culture sometimes want non-Christians to see that followers of Christ are not really that different from the rest of the world. Peter taught exactly the opposite: that genuine followers of Christ were supposed to live entirely different from the rest of the world and be aliens and strangers to everything that is relevant, important, and popular to the world. If you are not from here, how could you know about

---

[34] Joe Kohler, *The Forgotten Officer* (Bloomington, IN: WestBow Press, 2016), 3.

the popular culture? Christians have been called out of darkness and into light and ought to walk as children of light.[35]

Such hyper-contextualization is just another example of failed evangelism. Rather than trusting in the folly of the cross, it tries to dress up the gospel in worldly garbs. Rather than being a plain and unprofitable servant, it seeks to give the gospel messenger more influence than the gospel itself. At its root, it betrays a lack of faith in the Bible:

> Herein lay the tragedy of the Church's approach to the world in the twentieth century. Hesitant now to proclaim authoritative truth, she solaced herself in the face of men's unwillingness to receive Christianity with the idea that the old 'dogmatic approach' to evangelizing the earth was no longer legitimate...Disbelief in Scripture lay hidden beneath professed charity and tolerance.[36]

In contrast, Nathan Busenitz describes successful evangelism when saying, "Faithfulness, not temporal fame or visible fruitfulness, is His measure of success; and in the end, His assessment is the only one that matters."[37] In another place he says, "Our success is not determined by how the world responds to us in this life—whether with animosity, ambivalence, or applause—but by how Christ will evaluate us in the next."[38]

---

[35] Joe Kohler, *The Forgotten Officer* (Bloomington, IN: WestBow Press, 2016), 3-4.

[36] Iain H. Murray, *The Puritan Hope* (Carlisle, PA: The Banner of Truth, 1971), 229.

[37] Nathan Busenitz, "The Word of Truth in a World of Error," *Evangelism* (Nashville, TN: Thomas Nelson, 2011), 58.

[38] Busenitz, "The Word of Truth in a World of Error," *Evangelism*, 59.

The parable of the soils shows a sower who is simple and nameless (Mark 4:1-20). It shows seed that is simply seed, yet it is effective when sown into fertile soil. The seed does not need to be painted a fancy color. It does not need to be pumped with strange chemicals. It is good enough, and so is the gospel. It is the power of God that gives the growth, not the messenger, and not a seed that has been tampered with. This is why "we cannot finally judge the correctness of what we do in evangelism by the immediate response we see. It is important to understand this truth, because a failure to understand it can distract well-meaning churches into pragmatic, results-oriented endeavors and transform pastors into neurotic people-manipulators."[39]

When it comes to evangelism in the West, we see compromise, timidity, worldliness, and mush. This will never do. Like never before, Western Christianity is the foe of the culture. Have we not learned after two centuries of pragmatism that compromise does not "work"? That appeasing the world has backfired? It is time to decide if Christ is worth taking a stand for, and if so, with what do we fight? It is time to count the cost and to plunge into the trenches with nothing but the gospel. It is time to embrace being a mockery of the world. Spiritually speaking, it is time for dough-belly Christians to become battle-chiseled soldiers. Let us "stop regarding man in whose nostrils is breath" (Is. 2:22) and turn to God alone for how to do evangelism.

---

[39] Mark Dever, *Nine Marks of a Healthy Church* (Wheaton, IL: Crossway, 2000), 135.

PART THREE

THE COST

CHAPTER 8

What About Suffering?

THE CULTURE IN THE WEST is not "Christian." Such a statement should not be shocking. The cultures in most parts of the world are also not Christian. But for Christians who live in other parts of the world, severe persecution has long been underway, including martyrdom. But why do we not see such things in the West?

Admittedly there is still a thin veneer of Christian ideology that acts as a buffer against reckless persecution in the West, but this is rapidly eroding. There is an increase of arrests and lawsuits against Christians, but it is still mild compared to most of the world and even to what we see in church history. So are Western Christians compromising, unlike our brothers and sisters in other parts of the world? On the one hand we can praise God for the dearth of severe persecution taking place in the West. On the other hand, perhaps it is a mark against us, especially considering that most of our evangelism approaches to the culture are timid and pragmatic, which keeps persecution from being too intense. Perhaps this merely shows that we are not being as bold as we ought with the gospel.

Jesus talks about a rocky-soil person who, though he receives the word "with joy," endures until "tribulation or persecution arises on account of the word," which then causes him to "fall away" (Matt. 13:20-21). Biblical evangelism is unique because it necessarily brings tribulation and persecution from an unbelieving world. Although this is not the goal of evangelism, it is the consequence of it. This is why biblical evangelism is unpleasant to the flesh. This is also why so few Christians actually engage in biblical evangelism. We are fine being Christians until the Word causes trouble in our own lives, especially from other people, which is what biblical evangelism does. It flips the modern day message of comfort and luxury on its head, asking instead for confrontation. Biblical evangelism shows us how weak the flesh is, but also whether or not we are willing to deny ourselves, take up our crosses, and follow the Savior.

In the West, serious Christians are now discovering themselves to be the minority, and consequently, are being treated as the scum of the earth on an intensified level. Such persecution will only get worse against Christians who refuse to compromise their beliefs. Ultimately, if things continue as they are, Christians in the West will likely be killed for their faith. At the very least, Christians in the West will be jailed or sued for hate-speech or bigotry, which is already beginning to happen. They will be seen as rebels of the state. Fabrications and slander will infiltrate their households.

But horrible persecution is not the most alarming aspect of

such a season. What is far more troubling is that even before such persecution has reached a horrible pitch, unbiblical means of evangelism are largely in vogue in an attempt to keep suffering to a minimum. If we are unable to suffer for the sake of the gospel in a culture only beginning to present itself as hostile against biblical Christianity, what will happen later, when such rage against the gospel becomes feverish and violent? We have seen that unbiblical evangelism can be brought about by a desire for success, whether salvifically or in terms of reputation, but it can also be brought on by our fear of suffering.

Evangelism Often Leads to Suffering, Not Numbers

Why does the contemporary Western church equate evangelism with success, rather than with suffering? Why does the contemporary church assume that the behavior of a Christian will attract unbelievers to the faith, considering that Jesus, the epitome of good behavior, told us to expect the world's hatred, not their love, which was substantiated by His own death? Paul's life and letters also substantiate the reality that the world hates Christians. The popular phrase "use words if necessary" wrongly assumes that showing the love of Christ without sharing the gospel will "win" people to Christianity. But this is not Christianity, nor is it evangelism. Love is a compelling influence, undoubtedly, and it should mark the lives of every Christian. But holding back the content of the gospel from unbelievers is a kind of self-love or self-preservation, not love for one's neighbor. It is a technique that keeps the Christian from suffering, as are any other evangelism techniques that hold back the full counsel of the gospel, as has been argued.

With exception of modern Western society, evangelism and suffering have always gone hand in hand. Jesus spoke of the disciples' futures as including arrests, martyrdom, and assaults from their own family. It was spoken in a very plain and factual way. The disciples never protested against it. His meaning was unmistakable to them, which is remarkable considering their ordinary confusion over Jesus' teachings.

The early church experienced similar persecution, as did the true church in the Middle Ages at the hand of the Roman Catholics. During the Reformation in the West, Wycliffe, Jan Hus, Luther, Calvin, and the Puritans faced conflict without, fears within, especially as it related to advancing the gospel into unbelieving territory: "The Reformation was not merely about getting people to change religions or ecclesiastical affiliations. It was about bringing people to the true gospel of Jesus Christ so that they would find abiding life in Him."[1] Countless Christians died as a result. Many more suffered astonishing torture. So when did the mindset that evangelism should lead to success, not suffering, actually begin? When did Christians in Western society begin to assume that if evangelism was not seeing success, something is wrong? Or worse, that the Christians receiving such backlash must be too confrontational or mean-spirited?

In order to better examine biblical evangelism in the midst of suffering, let us turn again to an era of Christian history

---

[1] Wes Bredenhof, *To Win Our Neighbors for Christ* (Grand Rapids, MI: Reformation Heritage Books, 2012), 39.

where persecution against Christians was notoriously horrendous. During the first three centuries of the early church, in the face of real persecution, how often do we see them using pragmatic methods? Far from being pragmatists, the gospel message remained the same, beginning with Paul, despite the fact that such an uncompromised message is exactly the reason why persecution was so intense. Speaking of Paul's preaching in the marketplace, historian Ramsay MacMullen notes, "Paul and his fellow preachers had found it, or rather their words had made it, a dangerous business."[2] Continuing this theme of "dangerous words," MacMullen says elsewhere: "No one, of course, objected to their publicly discussing religion or exalting their own deity. A lot of that sort of discussion went on among non-Christians... What was rather bound to cause trouble was the express denial that the gods existed and that their images and services should be respected. Such talk was 'no-god-ly,' atheistic."[3] Michael Green says the same thing in *Evangelism in the Early Church*: "They were very bold about it, despite the opposition they encountered. There was no trace of compromise in their preaching.... Indeed they went out of their way to ridicule pagan Gods."[4]

Ironically, McMullen notes that the reason Christianity exploded in its first three centuries in comparison to other religions was this evangelistic culture that refused to quit or change course, even when suffering:

> The plain fact of evangelical effort in itself set Christianity apart and must be counted in any estimate of what

---

[2] Ramsay MacMullen, *Christianizing the Roman Empire* (New Haven, CT: Yale University, 1984), 105.

[3] MacMullen, *Christianizing the Roman Empire*, 105.

[4] Michael Green, *Evangelism in the Early Church* (Grand Rapids, MI: W. B. Eerdmans, 1970), 21.

happened. Belief in no other God but Yahweh entailed an obligation to speak in his praise and win over other worshippers to his service. That tradition, carried forward from Judaism, was also unique. Urgency, evangelism, and the demand that the believer deny the title of god to all but one, made up the force that alternative beliefs could not match.[5]

The early Christians recognized that any approach other than bold, confrontational evangelism would have been a denial of the very faith they claimed to believe in because of the subterfuge it would have required. "Had they been willing to practice their Christianity while remaining silent about other deities they could have had a comparatively safe passage. But they insisted that there was no other God than the Father of Jesus Christ...This was flying in the face of all convention and social propriety. It provoked savage persecution."[6]

Far from being concerned with salvific results, the Bible's approach to evangelism is aggressive and bold, especially in the Acts of the Apostles, where we see gospel proclamation that leads to devastating persecution and ridicule. Nothing changed in the early church, either. "The Christians were not persecuted because of their creed, but because of their universal claims."[7] It was not merely what they believed, but that they openly expressed such beliefs as binding on all individuals. They shoved their beliefs down people's throat, in other words. We don't like that language in today's church culture.

---

[5] MacMullen, *Christianizing the Roman Empire*, 110.

[6] Green, *Evangelism in the Early Church*, 21.

[7] Herbert B. Workman, *Persecution in the Early Church* (Bloomington, IL: Clearnote Press, 2014), 60.

We think it impolite to "push" our religion onto others. Not so with the early church. They were ridiculed and killed. They were seen as scandalous, precisely because they refused to be silent. Archibald Alexander notes,

> Christianity is so intolerant, that it will bear no other religion; it seeks to overthrow every other system. If it would have admitted the claims of other religions, it would have escaped persecution. But no; it denounced every other system and mode of worship as hateful to God, destructive to the soul...And every one now, whether male or female, bond or free, Jew or Greek, who professes Christianity, takes upon himself or herself the obligation to convert others to Christianity.[8]

The same is true today about those who actively evangelize with their mouths. Merely being a Christian generally won't bring about persecution in our culture. But once you unashamedly press the gospel onto others, there will be backlash. In our culture you can believe anything you want so long as you don't claim everyone else must believe it as well. Once the Christian declines to be tame in matters of evangelism, people are more likely to be upset than to be converted. However, this by no means indicates something is defective about the gospel or evangelism. It actually confirms the Bible to be true, since this is the reaction it promises from the world.

Had the early church been more pragmatic or seeker sensitive, the persecution would have been less intense. This is obvious. Had they been more quiet and cosmopolitan about

---

[8] Archibald Alexander, *Practical Truths* (Harrisonburg, VA: Sprinkle Publications, 1998), 32-33.

their faith, perhaps they would have found more peace among their neighbors. So why didn't they do it this way? Were they being foolhardy or unwise? The Western church today may say so, but what makes us think that the soft-peddled way we go about evangelism in the West is correct? Who could deny the magnetism of their approach, especially as compared to modern Christianity's? It brought about severe persecution and hatred of the world, but even in the eyes of their foes, who could deny that the gospel they preached must be real? What else could stimulate such an approach? The criticism so often heard today regarding bold, frontline evangelism was exactly the kind of evangelism we see the early church engaged in, which also brought an empire to its knees: "We sometimes think that relativism and pluralism are peculiar to our time. We feel it politically correct to adopt them. Not so the early Christians. They live in a world more relativist and far more pluralist than our own. And yet they would not make any compromise on this issue."[9]

So why do we see the early church boldly and even aggressively storming their culture with nothing but the gospel and intercessory prayer, whereas in our own climate, with far less persecution taking place, anyone who imitates the early church in this matter is condemned as too brash or too unloving? Perhaps the more dominant reason is fear of suffering: "We find it hard to be both loving and firm. We shy away from confrontation. We are embarrassed to claim that Jesus is the

---

[9] Timothy B. Bayly, "Foreword" to *Persecution in the Early Church* (Bloomington, IL: Clearnote Press, 2014), v.

only way. It is regarded as intolerant, narrow-minded and discourteous. But that is what our forebears did."[10]

Many pastors boldly proclaim the gospel in the church building. Many Christians speak boldly about the gospel while in the midst of other Christians. We have no problem denouncing other religions and unbiblical agendas in such arenas. But when we go into the world we no longer speak the same way. We are afraid of being seen as intolerant or mean-spirited. We are afraid of backlash from the culture. When we remember that many Christians condemn and criticize those who "too" boldly share the gospel or denounce unbiblical sins and worldviews, it is apparent that things have been inverted when comparing our approach to the early church. We might not face much persecution as a result, but neither do we see the spiritual impact that the early church had. This is especially stunning when we remember the early church did not have buildings on every corner nor material resources. What they had was a boldness that, though it brought about suffering, was also maintained in the face of suffering, which was more attractive than any friendship or kindness could have been.

To be fair, we should note that such a fear of suffering is not new to our Christian culture, even as it relates to compromising the gospel message. Paul dealt extensively with such a phenomenon in his letter to the Galatians. The church's fear of being ostracized or persecuted for the sake of justification by faith alone had led them to compromise. Even Peter was guilty. The problem was a fear of man, which in the Galatian church led to the demand that Gentile believers be circumcised, while

---

[10] Bayly, "Foreword" to *Persecution in the Early Church*, v.

in the realm of evangelism, it leads to approaches that defang the offense of the cross. The motive for both is "that they not be persecuted for the cross of Christ" (Gal. 6:12). To actually declare the full counsel of the gospel to an unbeliever often results in persecution against the messenger, which is the fruit of the unbeliever's hatred of the message. Paul himself came with "much fear and trembling" (1 Cor. 2:3), yet he still preached Christ and Him crucified. He never resorts to under-handed tactics. He sticks to bold gospel declaration, whether in conversation or in the open air, and it lead to persecution.

The gospel has always been an unwelcome message to the lost. The same is true in our own day. It involves God's judgment and the exclusivity of Christ. When it comes to sharing such a message, there are two options, both of which have confronted every believer since the days of Christ. We can either lay it all on the table, God's holiness, hell, the cross, all of it, and command the unbeliever to choose this day whom he will serve, knowing that it flies in the face of all convention, worldly wisdom, and social tact, yet declaring the message anyways because it is the method prescribed by God. Or we can water it down. We can soften its edge. We can hide some parts under a bushel, giving it piecemeal to the unbeliever. But in doing so we would show ourselves to no longer be serving God, but man (Gal. 1:10). The early church, by and large, believed the gospel alone was the power of God to save unbelievers (Rom. 1:16). They would have been appalled by the amount of pragmatic evangelism being done for the sake of removing the offense of the cross, since it was exactly that offense which caused them to suffer so much.

Despite the persecution against the early church, it is still a fact that the church attained a population of five million professing believers by the turn of the fourth century.[11] Such a statistic needs to be viewed with reservation, of course, since not all professing believers were true believers, as we see in our day as well. Also God pours out His Spirit in different ways during different times, so we can't say that if we follow the evangelism model of the early church we will see the same impact. Such numerical success should not be the point of evangelism, anyway, which is the point of this book. However, because the early church's evangelism was bold, frontline, and uncompromising—anything but pragmatic—God alone gets the glory for every conversion that took place. If the gospel had been compromised or distilled in a pragmatic way, man's ingenuity would have received the glory. We would praise the early church for their tact, rather than God for His faithfulness.

God blessed the simplicity of the gospel in the early church, as He promised He would. But God also blessed the church's suffering since it too abounded to His glory: "The capacity of Christians to face criticism, hatred, persecution and death not just with equanimity but with joy must have had a tremendous impact. We know it did. You could mow these Christians down, you could throw them to the lions, but you could not make them deny their Lord or hate their persecutors."[12]

Suffering Itself Is a Gospel Witness

When it comes to suffering, it is a gospel witness in itself. Is it possible, for example, that people could be saved from hearing about Christians suffering for their faith? Justin Martyr is an

[11] MacMullen, *Christianizing the Roman Empire*, 32.
[12] Workman, *Persecution in the Early Church*, 20.

example of this, who said about his pre-conversion days, "I myself, too, when I was delighting in the teachings of Plato, and heard the Christians slandered, and saw them fearless of death and of all things which are counted fearful, I understood."[13] In the footnote to this quote, Michael Green expounds on the context in which Justin was writing: "He understood from the way they met their deaths that the Christians could not be, as they were accused of being, living in wickedness and vice. But the impact of these deaths on him as a vindication of the doctrines they espoused is obvious."[14] In another place Green declares that the sufferings of Christians was the means for many converts in the early church: "The assurance and confidence of the Christians, who were quite willing to lose home, comfort, friends and even life itself in propagating their cause, won its share of converts."[15]

Perhaps this is what Paul meant when he said "that what has happened to me has really served to advance the gospel, so that it has become known throughout the whole imperial guard and to all the rest that my imprisonment is for Christ" (Phil. 1:13). The sufferings of Paul even encouraged others to go out and share their faith with more boldness, meaning that more evangelism was being done on account of it (Phil. 1:14). How different such an approach is from our day, when Christians in the West think that persecution and reproach can only bring shame to the gospel.

In the days of the early church, pagan religions were also willing to help the poor and set up institutions for social aid.

---

[13] Green, *Evangelism in the Early Church*, 200.

[14] Green, *Evangelism in the Early Church*, 435.

[15] Green, *Evangelism in the Early Church*, 176.

Pagans, too, loved one another. Some were probably very nice people, like many Buddhists, Muslims, and Roman Catholics. The question regarding Christianity's explosion in the early church is why did they see growth and not the pagans? The Christians could not have offered material or social comforts because they had none, nor would it have been wise to broadcast themselves through such means. They could not have promised protection against enemies like many pagan religions could. In fact, the opposite was the case. To become a Christian was to lose protection against enemies and to lose any social aid. These were not pragmatists. The only argument for pragmatism in the early Christian era would have been the miracles they performed, but even this can't explain why Christians attracted followers since pagans had miracle workers as well.

The only explanation is their different approaches to evangelism and the way God blessed it. No one else in the world, including ethnic Jews, could match the way the Christians went about proclaiming the gospel, and it came with both converts and suffering. The two went hand in hand. As pagans left their religions for Christianity, it created "waves of desperation" throughout the empire, which only led to more persecution. Christian evangelism caused spiritual "destruction" to the other religions, and it was done through the simple means of gospel proclamation and prayer: "It was this result, destruction, that non-Christians of the time perceived as uniquely Christian; and it was this result which in turn gave so grave a meaning, from the pagan point of view as well as the Christian, to the successive waves of persecution."[16]

---

[16] MacMullen, *Christianizing the Roman Empire*, 109.

This is just another reminder of why anything that attempts to soften or hide the realities of the gospel is unworthy of Jesus Christ. Gospel proclamation is a means for converting sinners. But also, those who hear about the messenger's suffering on account of the gospel will be likely to inquire more deeply into the Christian faith and why they were willing to go through such reproach. At the very least, the sufferings of the Christian will generate more boldness in other Christians, so that they then go out and share the gospel.

This shows us why evangelizing for the sake of "the one," as virtuous as it seems to be, can't be done in any reliable way, since God's work is often mysterious and not necessarily according to any kind of set pattern. Sometimes "the one" will be saved. Other times, "the one" won't be saved and there will be terrible persecution, which in turn might be used to save someone else after they hear about such persecution. Or it might not. Or it may be done to stimulate others to go and share the gospel which in turn, unbeknown to the Christian being persecuted, is used to save some. But even if none are saved, the most important thing of all is guaranteed—Christ's name is being preached, and hence, Christ receives glory.

Whether or not someone is saved, suffering for the sake of the gospel is a glorious testimony to the reality of God. So why are so many ministries and Christians horrified, it seems, of suffering? Why are so many ashamed when the lost are offended? Why are so many ashamed of losing their "good" reputation in the eyes of the world? Why do so many fear "bad reviews"? The main objective of many evangelism ministries seems to be keeping themselves safe from suffering, which they think will cast more attractive light on Christ. Biblical testimony and church history shows the opposite is true.

Paul addresses the same thing in 2 Corinthians 2:15-16: "For we are the aroma of Christ to God among those who are being saved and among those who are perishing, to one a fragrance from death to death, to the other a fragrance from life to life." Paul has already acknowledged that evangelism helps spread "the fragrance of the knowledge of him everywhere" (2 Cor. 2:14). Evangelism, and more specifically, the Christian who evangelizes, is like an offering of sweet incense to God. We evangelize to "those who are being saved" and likewise "to those who are perishing." When we evangelize, we please God regardless of whether or not "the one" is saved. We are "a fragrance from death to death" to those who are lost. The one evangelizing smells like death. The message itself is death. But what happens next marks the contrast between biblical evangelism and unbiblical evangelism. Biblical evangelism is sharing the gospel even if it only produces death. The one evangelizing won't change the gospel to make the odor more appealing. They won't try to spray it with pragmatic perfume or hide it under flesh-appealing paint. They won't dress it up in fancy garments in order to keep the corpse hidden from the unbeliever. Biblical evangelism is knowing that only God can change a person's view of the gospel, and it is His sovereign will alone to do so. Our job is to share it.

On the other hand, as Paul mentions one verse later, unbiblical evangelism will "peddle" the gospel in order to protect oneself against suffering. Such an approach "chops it up" in order to suppress its offence: "For we are not, like so many, peddlers of God's word, but as men of sincerity, as commissioned by God, in the sight of God we speak in Christ" (2 Cor. 2:17). Evangelism that deliberately keeps back the full gospel of God is a case of gospel-peddling, and it is often done out of fear of suffering.

Biblical Suffering[17]

We must expect opposition when evangelizing. "Jews demand signs and Greeks seek wisdom," but the one evangelizing must "preach Christ crucified, to the Jews a stumbling block and to the Greeks foolishness" (1 Cor. 1:23). The majority of people exposed to the gospel of Christ will reject it before it reaches their ears. The seed will fall on hard ground (Matt. 13:1-23). The one who presents the beauty of Christ will discover most are blind and unwilling to look upon Him. This is why the professing Christian who does not know his Bible will see "confrontational" evangelism as harmful or useless. But those who have studied the Bible, especially as it regards evangelism, will see that this kind of response corroborates perfectly with God's promise: "The natural man does not receive the things of the Spirit of God, for they are foolishness to him; nor can he know them, because they are spiritually discerned" (1 Cor. 2:14). Or again, "Our gospel is veiled...to those who are perishing, whose minds the god of this age has blinded, who do not believe, lest the light of the gospel of the glory of Christ, who is the image of God, should shine on them" (2 Cor. 4:3-4).

This is not to say that fear is unnatural and should be eliminated from the life of the believer. Rather, fear should drive

---

[17] The following two sections have been developed from *A Certain Sound: A Primer on Open Air Preaching*, written by Scott Smith and myself (Grand Rapids, MI: Reformation Heritage Books, 2019).

the believer to Christ for strength and wisdom. Fear can be valuable when it keeps us at the feet of our Savior. Paul himself was not above fear:

> What is particularly interesting about Paul's single-minded resolve to preach the undiluted gospel is his immediate admission that he struggled with the same feelings of apprehension and intimidation all of us experience when we contemplate our duty to proclaim it. As he reflected on his early ministry in Corinth, here is how he characterized it: "I was with you in weakness, in fear, and in much trembling" (1 Cor. 2:3).[18]

Peter also acknowledges that the Christian will suffer for the sake of righteousness (1 Pet. 3:8-17). He even claims that by doing so he "will be blessed." Peter encourages the Christian who evangelizes to "have no fear of them, nor be troubled, but in your hearts honor Christ the Lord as holy." Peter knew what it was to go into battle with the gospel. He was often in the trenches himself. In his early days he resorted to a literal, material sword against his enemies, hacking off ears without premeditation (John 18:10). His response to those who came to arrest Jesus must have been well-known since all the gospels contain it. Later in life, matured and battle-hardened, he went on to tell his readers to "not repay evil for evil or reviling for reviling, but on the contrary, bless, for to this you were called, that you may obtain a blessing" (1 Pet. 3:9).

He must have learned such meekness from spending time before the Lord, not only while Christ was on earth, but

---

[18] John MacArthur and Jesse Johnson, "Rediscovering Biblical Evangelism," *Evangelism* (Nashville, TN: Thomas Nelson, 2011), ix.

after His ascension. Consider the words of Christ himself on the subject:

> But I say to you who hear: Love your enemies, do good to those who hate you, bless those who curse you, and pray for those who spitefully use you. To him who strikes you on the one cheek, offer the other also. And from him who takes away your cloak, do not withhold your tunic either...But love your enemies, do good, and lend, hoping for nothing in return; and your reward will be great, and you will be sons of the Most High. For He is kind to the unthankful and the evil. Therefore be merciful, even as your Father also is merciful (Luke 6:27-36).

Paul also provides perhaps the best example of how to properly suffer when evangelizing. A man of hot blood, he never flinched when harassed by opponents. Stoned at Lystra, he was dragged away as though dead (Acts 14:19-23). When he came to his senses he did not stay down. He did not walk away. He returned to the city. In Ephesus, Paul's companions had to hold him back from entering the theater when the city was in an uproar because of the gospel (Acts 19:8-41). Paul was not one to avoid conflict, nor was he ignorant of the battles of evangelism: "When we came to Macedonia, our bodies had no rest, but we were troubled on every side. Outside were conflicts, inside were fears" (2 Cor. 7:5). Yet later in life Paul exhorts Timothy to be kind and gentle when dealing with opponents: "And a servant of the Lord must not quarrel but be gentle to all, able to teach, patient, in humility correcting those who are in opposition" (2 Tim. 2:24-25). Notice Paul and Peter both employ the word "gentle." These men were not effeminate. They were men's men. Yet they emphasize that the Christian must be gentle, even when suffering.

Paul goes a step further by saying "the Lord's servant must not be quarrelsome" (2 Tim. 2:24). Quarreling is a constant temptation when suffering for the gospel. Opponents will heckle the Christian in every way imaginable. Abuse will be thundered against the Lord's servant. Attacks and filthy words will be hurled against him. His intelligence will be insulted. They will spit on him. They will throw coffee and beer and soda on him. They will yank the Bible from his hand and chew up the pages. Some may deck him in the jaw. Some will write defaming articles about him or castigate him on social media. But Paul essentially says, "It doesn't matter—be kind to everyone." In his letter to the Romans he repeats the words of the Lord: "Bless those who persecute you; bless and do not curse" (Rom. 12:14). He exhorts the church to leave revenge to God and to overcome evil with good, not evil (Rom. 12:19). Paul exhorts the church in Colossae in a similar way: "Walk in wisdom toward those who are outside, redeeming the time. Let your speech always be with grace, seasoned with salt, that you may know how you ought to answer each one" (Col. 4:5-6). In other words, it is not only when everything is going our way that the Christian must be kind, gentle, and wise towards his opponents. It is every time we suffer.

Jesus also knew the battles of evangelism. He was the greatest one to ever do it. He knew the grind of heralding truth to all who have ears and to those who don't. Our Lord was tempted in every way we are, yet was without sin (Heb. 4:15). He was threatened with stones, almost thrown off a cliff, abandoned by disciples and family, yet He remained meek and lowly of heart (Matt. 11:29).

What is more, He continued to believe in the power of the gospel. Christ was fully God in every way, but Christ was fully man as well. Christ was threatened by false accusations, mobs that tried to kill Him, and the devil. He was betrayed by the religious establishment, betrayed by His own nation, without bed or pillow or chariot, yet He commands us to "love your enemies, do good to those who hate you, bless those who curse you, and pray for those who spitefully use you" (Luke 6:27-29).

The Christian does well to share the gospel in the highways and hedges. But is he obedient to the more difficult task of loving his enemy or doing good to those who hate him, especially when it causes intense suffering? Does he bless those who curse him and pray for those who mistreat him? Jesus asked His disciples, "But why do you call me 'Lord, Lord' and not do the things which I say?" (Luke 6:46). The same could be said for the Christian who responds to his opponents with the wrong spirit. The Christian will be sharing the gospel to people whose father is "the devil" (John 8:44-45). How does he expect them to respond? They will announce themselves as his enemy in every way they can. The Christian must expect it. But how will the Christian respond when it hurts? How does he respond when the attacks are personal? "If anyone among you thinks he is religious, and does not bridle his tongue but deceives his own heart, this one's religion is useless" (James 1:26).

Examples abound in church history of Christians responding both correctly to opposition and at times acting in the flesh. Research in this area can be a great encouragement and refiner for us. For example, in the first two centuries of the church, sharing the gospel in public brought the same response as it does today: "The mockery, the joking, the heckling, even the physical danger to the preacher which he describes must have happened on countless open air platforms."[19] But the hope and prayer of every Christian should not be, "Lord keep me from danger" or "Lord keep me from suffering," but rather, "Lord, when danger and suffering come, fill my soul 'sweetly' with your Spirit."[20]

The True Danger—Ourselves

The Christian must guard against a bitter spirit when evangelizing, especially when it causes backlash. Sharing the gospel to the lost, especially our family members, can callous the hearts of the most mature. The Christian will engage the worst demons in the world when evangelizing. This can numb even the most compassionate of believers. An awareness of the danger will help us be constant in prayer against such deadening effects. Like all of the most heinous sins, bitterness takes place slowly. The Christian won't wake up one morning and suddenly be bitter towards the lost. In the beginning most Christians will be tender and patient when evangelizing. They will reason with the lost like a mother dealing with a child. But slowly the patience wanes. Each day the Christian is cloaked with a thin sheet of resentment. The blasphemies of the lost begin to wear on him. Eventually he sees the lost through a lens of burning hatred rather than love. He forgets that apart from the grace of God he would be just as lost. He gets to the point where he is no longer concerned about their souls. He sees evangelism as a duty, something to check off the list, not as good news for sinners. This happens unconsciously. The Christian likely will never notice it. This is the danger. This

---

[19] Green, *Evangelism in the Early Church*, 306.
[20] John Morgan Jones and William Morgan, *The Calvinistic Methodist Fathers of Wales*, vol. 1 (Carlisle, PA: The Banner of Truth Trust, 1890), 78-79.

is why the Christian needs to be held accountable to his church and other brothers. In some cases, even if he does notice it or is told about it by others, his hatred and bitterness for the lost will be so great that it won't bother him. He will blame the lost rather than repent and ask God for more tenderness. This is a danger for every Christian when evangelizing. He is constantly battling the evils of this world. He deals constantly with people who hate him and hate God. The Christian must constantly be in prayer and self-examination. He must be the most prayerful saint in the city.

This is also why the Christian must constantly pray for more love towards the lost. The flesh won't do it. The old man won't want it. But "He who is in you is greater than he who is in the world" (1 John 4:4), which is why we can be constant to engage in biblical evangelism, even if none are saved. Robert Flockhart of Edinburgh was known for his fiery temperament, yet consider Spurgeon's description of him, with which we close the chapter, exhorting the reader to go and do likewise:

Though a lesser light, he was a constant one, and a fit example to the bulk of Christ's street witnesses. Every evening, in all weathers and amid many persecutions, did this brave man continue to speak in the street for forty-three years. Think of that, and never be discouraged. When he was tottering to the grave the old soldier was still at his post. "Compassion to the souls of men drove me," said he, "to the streets and lanes of my native city, to plead with sinners and persuade them to come to Jesus. The love of Christ constrained me."[21]

---

[21] Spurgeon, *Lectures to My Students*, 125.

CHAPTER 9

When Christians Get Arrested[1]

PEOPLE ARE INCREASINGLY JAILED, fined, or fired in the West for sharing the gospel, but it is still the exception, not the norm. Whenever it does happen, Christians in general usually fault the one evangelizing for "getting into trouble" or being "insubordinate" to officials. Christians in the West often seem outraged that someone would dare elicit the scorn of public officials or society to the extent that they would actually be put into jail. The reason Christians in the West respond this way to evangelism that causes "trouble" is because Western Christianity does not experience much suffering. However, Western Christianity does not experience much suffering because we are reluctant to be bold or outspoken with the gospel. Some may assume this is a blessing. It is actually the opposite.

---

[1] Parts of this chapter has been developed from *A Certain Sound: A Primer on Open Air Preaching*, written by Scott Smith and myself (Grand Rapids, MI: Reformation Heritage Books, 2019).

When it comes to evangelism, how should we respond to police officers and authorities, especially since it is increasingly an issue for those who bring the gospel outside church walls? What about employers and jobs when it comes to evangelism, since it is already taboo to talk about Christ at work? "Proselytizing" is still legal in the West, but with increasing reservations and limits. What happens when Western society actually bans public evangelism since it is intolerant or offends other parties? In the United Kingdom this restriction already exists when it comes to preaching or even quoting the Bible on the issue of homosexuality.[2] To say anything that offends another person, even if it is a direct quotation from the Bible, will make you liable to arrest, paying a fine, or being forced to leave the premises for a fixed period of time. The same is true in Switzerland, where "homophobia" is an official crime.[3] America is not far behind when it comes to such restrictions, even if on paper there is more freedom.

But do such restrictions mean that evangelism should cease? Are we to stop sharing what the Bible says regarding such topics as hell, homosexuality, abortion, or the command to repent and believe the gospel, since the West is increasingly deciding that to do so is illegal? This is not to suggest that the topic of homosexuality or abortion should be brought up every time we evangelize, nor are these topics the essential message of the gospel. The point is that if negative views about such issues are already deemed criminal, it won't be long until any mention of sin or judgement is also made illegal.

---

[2] "The Hate Police Are Now Here," The Wee Flea, accessed February 21, 2019, https://theweeflea.com/2018/10/02/the-hate-police-are-now-here/.

[3] "Switzerland votes overwhelmingly to jail citizens for 'homophobia,' 'transphobia,'" Life Site News, accessed February 21, 2019, https://www.lifesitenews.com/news/switzerland-votes-overwhelmingly-to-jail-citizens-for-homophobia-transphobi.

We know the Christian is required by God to be "subject to the governing authorities" (Rom. 13:1). It is no coincidence these words were written to believers in Rome at the height of emperor worship and other pagan rituals. The Christian must not "resist" the governing authorities, since doing so would be to resist the authorities that "God has appointed" (Rom. 13:2) to bear the sword. But notice Paul's argument pivots on the assumption that the governing authorities "are not a terror to good works, but to evil" (Rom. 13:3). So what happens when the governing authorities do become terrors to good works or good behavior, as outlined in Scripture? What happens when the governing authorities attempt to resist the Christian from sharing or preaching the gospel in public? Paul says the authorities bear the sword for the purpose of carrying out God's wrath "on the wrongdoer" (Rom. 13:4). What happens when the sword comes against those sharing Christ in public? What happens when the Christian is treated as the wrongdoer, simply because he is opening his mouth about God at work or with a neighbor? Surely there is a perversion of justice in this case, but how should the Christian respond?

Unfortunately for those in the USA, it is becomingly increasingly pointless to appeal to the United States Constitution and the protection it promises under the First Amendment. The Christian will encounter officers, employers, and a society who in general no longer see the Constitution as authoritative. For Western Christians outside the USA, it has long been the case that "free speech" laws are irrelevant considering all of the exceptions that come with them. The ability of the Western Christian to voice his beliefs in public is already complicated. Jeremy Walker describes this erosion in *The Brokenhearted Evangelist*:

"Legislators promote godlessness on a grand scale, not just at a tangent to God's Word but utterly regardless of it. In the modern West, civil statutes that once were founded on God's moral law enshrined in the Ten Commandments are being swept away and replaced with the concoctions of the moment."[4]

So what should the Christian do? What happens when it becomes illegal to share the gospel, as it now is in most places of work or education and even in many public forums? Does defying such a rule go against Paul's commands in Romans 13? Are there times when disobeying authority is not only acceptable but even required of the Christian, especially as it pertains to evangelism? Or should we come up with other, more underhanded approaches to evangelism for the sake of propriety and civil decency?

First of all, our authority and commission to evangelize comes from Christ, not the government. All authority in the universe belongs to Christ, who has told us to "Go, therefore," and bring the gospel to a lost world. The Christian should be respectful at all times to the governing authorities, in so far as they are human beings and made in the image of God. If he is to be arrested, let him conduct himself with gentleness and respect. If he is to defy the authorities, let him do so with all the meekness of Jesus, who was "afflicted, yet He opened not His mouth; He was led as a lamb to the slaughter, and as a sheep before its shearers is silent, so He opened not His mouth (Is. 53:7). The Christian should never intentionally provoke the authorities for the sake of being arrested or for any other purpose. But to say he should cave to the perversion of justice or the corruption of a country's

---

[4] Jeremy Walker, *The Brokenhearted Evangelist* (Grand Rapids, MI: Reformation Heritage Books, 2012), 12.

agenda against God is likewise unbiblical. We are told to preach the gospel to all creation (Mark 16:15). If the Christian is arrested for preaching or sharing the gospel, he follows others who have been similarly treated, including the Apostle Paul, who wrote Romans 13. In such a case he should not be ashamed.

To consider this in light of church history, John Calvin states that "we are subject to the men who rule over us, but only in the Lord. If they command anything against Him let us not pay the least regard to it."[5] Calvin was not an anti-government radical, nor did he believe the Christian should whimsically throw off the restraints of even a tyrannical ruler. Instead, recognizing the tension between the Romans 13 mandate to "be subject unto the higher powers" and Acts 5:29 mandate "to obey God rather than men," both Calvin and Luther agree that allowances to such obedience must be made.

Luther provides two specific examples of when disobedience is permitted. The first is when the government calls on the citizen to participate in or commit a harm against his neighbor. The second "is when the secular powers step out of their proper realm and presume to prescribe matters of belief and worship contrary to God's Word."[6] Outlawing evangelism in public, for instance, would fall under the category of issuing a restraint "contrary to God's Word," and in a sense it could be argued it is also harmful to our neighbor, since the gospel alone is the power of God to save him. In this case, the Christian would not be obligated to obey.

---

[5] John Calvin, *Institutes of the Christian Religion*, Ed. John McNeill (Louisville, KY: Westminster Press, 1960), IV., xx. 32.

[6] Duncan B. Forrester, "Martin Luther and John Calvin," *History of Political Philosophy*, Ed. Leo Strauss and Joseph Cropsey (Chicago: University of Chicago Press, 1963), 340.

The Early Church's Willful Neglect of Authority

Even in Scripture we see this same approach to the civil government. Christians who were arrested on a regular basis played a primary role in the New Testament church's foundation. Consider Peter and John, for example, in the early part of the Acts of the Apostles:

Now as they spoke to the people, the priests, the captain of the temple, and the Sadducees came upon them, being greatly disturbed that they taught the people and preached in Jesus the resurrection from the dead. And they laid hands on them, and put them in custody until the next day, for it was already evening (Acts 4:1-3).

Note the officials were "greatly disturbed" because they were teaching the people and proclaiming Jesus. Let this be the reason the Christian is arrested or fired. The proclamation of Jesus was what antagonized the officials. Afterwards, when Peter and John were told to stop preaching Christ, they declined to obey: "'Whether it is right in the sight of God to listen to you more than to God, you judge. For we cannot but speak the things which we have seen and heard'" (Acts 4:19-20). Rather than being daunted by public officials and criticism from the community, they went on to pray for increased boldness: "Now, Lord, look on their threats, and grant to Your servants that with all boldness they may speak Your word" (Acts 4:29). The Christian should share the cross without fear of public officials. He should share the gospel without concern for his wellbeing. He should preach without concern of arrest.

Preach Christ and Him crucified until the whole world either comes against you or is saved.

One chapter later the apostles are arrested again. Far from submitting to unlawful authorities, God Himself sends an angel to deliver them from jail. Far from the angel telling them to stop preaching, he commands them to "'go, stand in the temple and speak to the people all the words of this life.' And when they heard that, they entered the temple early in the morning and taught" (Acts 5:20-21). Notice it is God who is directing the apostles to defy public officials. Again the apostles are arrested. Agai, they are told to stop preaching by the authorities. Again the apostles defy this command: "But Peter and the other apostles answered, 'We ought to obey God rather than men'" (Acts 5:29). What is more astonishing, Peter goes on to preach Christ to the officials who just told him to stop preaching. The response of the authorities is starkly familiar to the reaction towards many Western Christians who continue to share the gospel in public, whether on a street corner, at college, or at work: "When they heard this, they were furious and plotted to kill them" (Acts 5:33).

Stephen is killed two chapters later for preaching Christ, which is a reminder that the church was built by the blood and, to a degree, the arrests of Christians. It is worth asking how modern Christians would react if other Christians were killed for sharing the gospel. Would modern Christians condemn them as unloving or unwise, seeing the provocation it caused? Would they encourage more pragmatism or relational models, hoping to lighten the offense? The early church never seems to consider such a move. We saw earlier that the church father Cyprian "even dared the authorities to arrest him as he preached in the market place during a period of persecution."[7] Although not every circumstance will call for such an action, we should appreciate his bold gospel preaching and his refusal to shrink back from suffering. The early church was "not anxious to run counter to the law and customs of the Empire; they were, in fact, unanimous in upholding them. But if at any time such law and customs came into conflict with the will of God, as interpreted by themselves and their standards, they must obey God rather than man."[8]

Evangelism's Uniqueness

To consider this from another perspective, how would Christians in the West respond if it suddenly became illegal to meet together for church or to study the Scriptures or attend prayer meetings? Would we do so anyway? Or would we stop meeting together, knowing that if we did, our freedom or perhaps our bank account could be compromised? Perhaps our family would be put at risk. Perhaps we could lose our lives.

This scenario is not exactly hypothetical. Such a day is likely on the horizon in the West. But why would it be different when it comes to evangelism? It is possible to meet in secret when it comes to worship and Bible studies, without society knowing about it. But evangelism necessarily involves the unbelieving community to know what we believe, including the offensive parts, since it is the unbelieving persons of society we are called to evangelize. This is what makes such a scenario very different. Evangelism requires the Christian to confront the worldview

---

[7] Michael Green, *Evangelism in the Early Church*, (Grand Rapids, MI: Wm. B Eerdmans Publishing Company, 1970), 304.

[8] Green, *Evangelism in the Early Church*, 144.

of an unbelieving person with the truth of the gospel, which is why the one evangelizing will be the first to see persecution and retaliation from society. We are commanded to evangelize. We do not have the luxury of simply stopping the work when it becomes illegal or uncomfortable. Not to mention that if we desire society to change or become more lenient toward Christians, what else but conversions will make this happen? And how will people be converted unless someone is speaking to them about Christ?

In most places in the West it is forbidden to proselytize at work, for instance. But the workplace has always been one of the primary places of evangelism for Christians both today and in the early church: "The chief agents in the expansion of Christianity appear not to have been those who made it a profession...but men and women who carried on their livelihood in some purely secular manner and spoke of their faith to those they met in this natural fashion."[9] If we are not evangelizing at work, we lose one of our primary opportunities to share the gospel with the lost.

Discretion should be advised, of course, since the author is not advocating for employees to use time on the clock to evangelize. Christians at work are being paid to work, which does not give them license to steal (in the form of time). Having a good work ethic will complement any gospel witness, while having a poor work ethic will compromise it. But most jobs provide excellent evangelism opportunities during breaks, lunch, or before and after hours. We must take advantage of every opportunity we have to speak Christ unto the lost,

---

[9] Kenneth S. Latourette, *A History of the Expansion of Christianity* (New York: Harper, 1944), 1:230.

regardless of the reaction, so long as it does not conflict with other God-given responsibilities that we have.

Be Prepared to Stand Alone

Paul was ready to go to prison even if it meant his death, as he states before going to Jerusalem for the final time (Acts 21:13). In the same verse we see the companions of Paul acting in a very relatable way. They are weeping. They are urging Paul to turn back. They are desperately insisting he avoid the trouble of such a decision. But Paul, knowing that arrest awaited him, refused to take their advice. The same is true today for those who boldly evangelize the lost. Other Christians beg them to stop or to think about the hardship it might bring to family or reputation. What if he gets fired? What if he gets thrown into jail? They urge caution and apathy. Perhaps they twist the Scriptures to make it seem less demanding about our duty to evangelize. But Paul's example shows us we are to fix our eyes on Jesus and buckle down even harder, regardless of the outcome, since Christ is worthy to suffer for. At the end of the day we are given a command to share the gospel, regardless of the cost. The more people who hear the gospel, the better. When the Christian is arrested, he should share the gospel in jail. He should preach Christ to all who have ears.

Decades of compromise to unlawful authorities have greatly reduced the rights of Christians in the West. Moreover, centuries have passed without Western Christians suffering very much when evangelizing. This has caused our notion of suffering to become very effeminate and timid, especially when it comes to civil authorities. They are supposed to be for us, not against us, and for hundreds of years this was usually the case. Not so anymore. It is time we get past such unreal expectations. The days are coming when Christians will go to jail or get fired for evangelizing, or they will simply stop evangelizing. Perhaps that day is already here. Either way, now is the time the Christian "obey God rather than men" (Acts 5:29) and continue to share Christ even if it leads to difficult repercussions.

Christian Unity in Face of Arrest

It would be improper to end such a chapter without a loving exhortation to Christians. On the one hand, we should never intentionally get arrested. The example of Irenaeus daring authorities to arrest him should probably not be imitated. But on the other hand, when Christians are arrested while evangelizing, we should be more scrupulous and considerate before criticizing or disciplining them. Christians and church leadership are far too quick to ostracize a brother or sister when it comes to arrests or trouble while evangelizing, even though Peter takes the opposite view: "Yet if anyone suffers as a Christian, let him not be ashamed, but let him glorify God in this matter" (1 Pet. 4:16).

The days we are living in are very similar to Peter's and the other early disciples. The West is becoming more and more like the Roman Empire. We are free to believe whatever we want, so long as we don't make it public, and so long as we don't make it binding on others. Defying such a mantra is what usually generates police involvement. This is exactly the scenario that the early church faced.

Perhaps the only encouraging part about the increase of

arrests while evangelizing in the West is the almost equal increase of such crimes being dropped once they reach court. This in itself should give Christians pause before criticizing someone for being arrested while evangelizing. That being said, eventually, such crimes will not be dropped if the current trend of cultural animosity towards the gospel continues. The crimes will stick, and the penalties will become harsher. But it doesn't mean the Christian is wrong for such a reaction to his evangelism, assuming his doctrine and approach are biblical. Eventually, unless there is a drastic shift in the West, it will be wrong not to be arrested, considering how sensitive the culture is becoming when it comes to the exclusivity of Christianity.

Being arrested would be sinful if the motive was carnal or selfish. However, in the scenarios we are considering, what is at stake is the gospel, and more importantly the glory of God that is conveyed whenever the gospel is communicated to the lost. For us to cease sharing the gospel simply because the authorities demand it would be to repudiate the primary source that God has always used to shower His riches across the earth. It would eliminate the means that God has always used to save the lost. It would remove the source that God has always used to build His church. The reason why liberal churches so often decline in numbers is because, quite simply, they don't evangelize. They don't have a literal view of hell. They don't have an exclusive view of religion. The biblical Christian does, and it should impel us to go forth and share the realities of hell and the beauty of the cross with the world, whether or not they want to hear it.

The fate of liberal churches awaits every church that ceases to evangelize, regardless of the motive. On the other hand, the fate of the early church awaits every Christian who evangelizes boldly. In every century, God has had persons proclaiming the gospel in the face of horrendous persecution, including arrests, and yet in every century God continues to build His kingdom on earth.

CHAPTER 10

A Glimmer of Hope

A GLANCE AT CHURCH HISTORY shows that the kind of drought we are experiencing in the West is not exactly new, nor should we assume that it will persist to "the end of time." On the contrary, we should expect God at any moment to pour out His spirit and revive dry bones. While most historical attention is given to epochs of revival, Thomas Boston complained of barren scenes in 1699, thirty-five years before the First Great Awakening:

> This day seems to be a day of darkness and gloominess; the glory is departed even to the threshold of the temple. We may call ordinances Ichabod; and name the faithful preachers of Scotland no more Naomi, but Mara, for the Lord deals bitterly with them, in so much forsaking his ordinances as at this day. The Lord hath forsaken them in great measure, as to success attending their labours. They

toil all the night; but little or nothing is caught; few or none can they find to come into the net...O my soul, what may be the cause of this, why does my preaching so little good?[1]

It probably never entered Boston's mind that God was going to save an ample crop of souls in the West, in part through his toil. The same could be seen in the *Memoir of Rice* about a Minister named Matthew Lyle, who was "converted in the revival of 1789 and spent all his ministry in Virginia, often afraid that he was accomplishing little." In 1828, after Lyle had died, a genuine work of God broke out in Virginia, and it was said about Lyle's labor three decades prior: "Much that our valued friend, Mr Lyle, did in the way of sowing seed, is now springing up, and producing a glorious harvest."[2]

The Western world saw revival in the middle ages, which we now call the Reformation. It happened again in the eighteenth century under Jonathan Edwards and George Whitefield. The nineteenth century West also saw large outpourings of the Holy Spirit. If God has done it in the past, who is to say He won't do it again in our day, using our generation as a catalyst? And even if we don't see revival in our day, we could be the ones who plow and sow so that the next generation can reap a harvest. Without a Wycliff or a Hus, you don't have a Luther or a Calvin. Some plant, some water, but God gives the increase (1 Cor. 3:6). "One sows and another reaps" is a law in Christ's kingdom (John 4:37).

The West has been overrun by paganism and unbelief. It is a

---

[1] Thomas Boston, *The Art of Man-Fishing*, (Ross-shire, Scotland: Christian Focus Publications, 1998), 17-18.

[2] Iain H. Murray, *Revival & Revivalism* (Carlisle, PA: The Banner of Truth, 1994), 385.

secular culture. God is irrelevant in the minds of most people. We see few conversions. We see statistics showing increases in atheism, agnosticism, and false religions.[3] And yet, at the end of the day, this is nothing new, nor should it keep us from being urgent in our evangelism. David Livingstone, missionary to Africa's heart of darkness in the 1800s, reminds us in his journals that "missionaries in the midst of masses of heathenism seem like voices crying in the wilderness—like Reformers before the Reformation. But future missionaries will see conversions follow every sermon. We prepare the way for them. May they not forget the pioneers who worked in the thick gloom with few rays to cheer, except such as flow from faith in God's promises!"[4]

One of the advantages of living in a secular culture is that we can no longer assume most people have heard the gospel. We are starting fresh. Pastor Joe Kohler said the same thing after spending a year evangelizing door to door and in downtown areas in one North American city: "It is astonishing how many people we meet who have never heard the basic content of the gospel. We have had churches in this area for decades, but still, the people are perishing in ignorance of the gospel. How can this be?"[5] This is advantageous because it means most people have never directly rejected the biblical gospel, either. Romans 1 shows that all are guilty and without excuse

---

[3] For examples of this see, "Is America becoming Godless? The number of people who have no religion has risen 266 percent—one third of the population—in three decades," *The Daily Mail*, conducted by General Social Survey. Last accessed April 5, 2019. www.dailymail.co.uk/news/article-6886705/Is-America-Godless-number-people-no-religion-rose-266-three-decades.html; "Survey: There are now as many Americans who claim no religion as there are evangelicals and Catholics," *CNN*. Last accessed April 13, 2019. www.cnn.com/2019/04/13/us/no-religion-largest-group-first-time-usa-trnd/index.html.

[4] Iain H. Murray, *The Puritan Hope* (Carlisle, PA: The Banner of Truth, 1971), 182.

[5] Joe Kohler, *The Forgotten Officer* (Bloomington, IN: WestBow Press, 2016), 57.

for their rebellion against God, but we still have a fresh opportunity to get the gospel to people who have never been confronted by it, unlike a generation or two ago, when we could assume most had heard the gospel in some form or another. Our culture is so thoroughly pagan that we are truly living in unreached territory. We could assume that the percentage who have heard the biblical gospel in the West is probably in the single digits.

Consider Jesus' great lesson on evangelism. He goes to the disciples after they had toiled all night for fish but caught nothing. They are tired and discouraged. He tells them to cast the net on the other side of the boat. Peter even says, "But we've fished all night and caught nothing" (Luke 5:5). He is implying that having seen no success previously, there won't be any success the next time either. But despite the mild protest, off they go, throwing the net out on the other side. They did not say to Jesus, "But you're a carpenter, not a fisherman." They knew who the Lord of the Harvest was. They trusted His sovereignty and they obeyed His orders. They were blessed with a great catch. Who is to say it won't be the same for us the next time we go forth to evangelize?

Who Should Be Evangelizing?

Ephesians 4 tells us that all Christians should be engaged in ministry, which includes evangelism. Christ tells his disciples to go into the world with the gospel. Every Christian has a sphere of relationships and opportunities that no other Christian in the world has. If the Christian refuses to share the gospel in such spheres and to such people, who will do it? The

Mormons? The Roman Catholics? The fact that Christians are not called to leave the world for a monastery or desert should be a reminder that one of our purposes in the world is to evangelize the lost in accordance with the God-decreed schedules and relationships we have.

Although planned or intentional evangelism is great, the reality is, Christians have a host of daily evangelism opportunities. What is difficult, however, is the inevitable confrontation which evangelism causes, especially with the people we know. But we are still called to do it, remembering that Jesus has all authority in heaven and earth, so we "go, therefore." We must speak about Christ to those contacts He has given us, using the gospel and intercessory prayer as our primary instruments. We are a peculiar people, after all, and must be ready and even eager to meet a storm of hatred at any time.

The same was true of the early church, whose growth came mostly through ordinary Christians sharing the gospel in their everyday environments: "Where, then, could believers make contact with unbelievers to win them over? Surely the answer must somehow lie where the Christians themselves direct our attention...in quite obscure settings of everyday."[6] Or again, "Being excluded from the normal social gatherings, their points of contact with non-Christians lay quite inevitably at street corners or at places of employment, or in the working quarters of dwellings."[7] The historian goes so far as to say that "evangelizing in private settings" was one of the most influential contexts for bringing about conversions to the Christian

---

[6] Ramsay MacMullen, *Christianizing the Roman Empire* (New Haven, CT: Yale University, 1984), 37.

[7] MacMullen, *Christianizing the Roman Empire*, 40.

religion "en masse."[8] Or again, consider the words of Celsus, a second century non-Christian writing about how Christians evangelized in his day:

> In private houses also we see wool-workers, cobblers, laundry-workers, and the most illiterate and bucolic yokels, who would not dare to say anything at all in front of their elders and more intelligent masters. But whenever they get hold of children in private and some stupid women with them, they let out some astounding statements as, for example, that they must not pay attention to their father and school-teacher, but must obey them instead; they say that these talk nonsense and have no understanding, and that in reality they neither know nor are able to do anything good, but are taken up with mere empty chatter. But they alone, they say, know the right way to live, and if the children would believe them, they would become happy and make their home happy as well...But, if they like, they should leave father and their schoolmasters, and go alone with the women and little children who are their playfellows to the wooldresser's shop, or to the cobbler's or the washerwoman's shop, that they may learn perfection. And by saying this they persuade them.[9]

Most Christians in the early church reserved their evangelism "to private houses," which was "the chief locus of conversion."[10] There were few missionaries. In fact, missionaries are rarely mentioned at all after the New Testament record.

---

[8] MacMullen, *Christianizing the Roman Empire,* 29.

[9] MacMullen, *Christianizing the Roman Empire,* 37.

[10] MacMullen, *Christianizing the Roman Empire,* 111.

Christians by necessity had to keep a low profile. Celsus even "reminds his readers, too, of the dangers entailed in open preaching."[11] This does not mean evangelism wasn't being done. It is clear from the growth of the church that widespread evangelism was taking place. It just shows how important every Christian is to the work of evangelism, whether or not they are ordained ministers, and how often God uses such people to add to His church. But such persons will still face persecution if they are faithful to evangelize in a biblical way: "Persecution, then, is not incidental to prophesying (preaching) but an ordained element of the prophet's life. And he who witnesses for Christ and His evangel is a prophet. If he truly loves Christ, as he must, persecution will not deter him from witnessing."[12]

Believers are called to profess the name of Christ to the lost. Backlash against such persons has always been the norm. And yet, "a silent prophet is unimaginable," regardless of the persecution it may bring. This is one way to understand Christ's promise that "everyone who acknowledges me before men I also will acknowledge before my father who is in heaven, but whoever denies me before men, I also will deny before my father who is in heaven" (Matt. 10:32-33). The next verse promises that Jesus did not come to bring peace to the earth, but a sword (Matt. 10:34).[13]

To know that every Christian should be evangelizing can cause disturbance and shame for many Christians. Most of us

---

[11] MacMullen, *Christianizing the Roman Empire*, 111.

[12] Herbert B. Workman, *Persecution in the Early Church* (Bloomington, IL: Clearnote Press, 2014), 104.

[13] Wes Bredenhof, *To Win Our Neighbors for Christ* (Grand Rapids, MI: Reformation Heritage Books, 2012), 49.

feel inadequate when it comes sharing the gospel. But consider the demoniac, who was told right after his conversion to go and tell all about what Jesus had done for him (Mark 5:19). He knew enough of the gospel to share it with others. Rather than being afraid to do so, his overwhelming love for Christ drove him on to do it. "That is precisely why new Christians are often the most passionate evangelists. Without any training or encouragement whatsoever, they can be amazingly effective in bringing others to Christ. They are not obsessed with technique or stymied by fear of rejection. The sheer, grand glory of the gospel fills their hearts and their vision, and they want to talk to everyone about it."[14]

Evangelism is pointing people to Christ, and if a person has been saved, they know enough about Christ to talk about Him with others. "In the sphere to which God has appointed you (in consideration of your calling, circumstances, gifts, and graces), are you prepared to speak a word for Jesus Christ? If you are not, it is sin. It is sin to keep silent when those around us are dying."[15] John MacArthur's congregation provides an example remarkably similar to the evangelism scene in the early church, and it is one that all of our churches should strive to emulate:

> People in our church witness to their neighbors, coworkers, other parents in Little League, friends at school, people in the markets, their doctors, their attorneys, and everyone they meet. And over the years the Lord has blessed that

---

[14] John MacArthur and Jesse Johnson, "Rediscovering Biblical Evangelism," *Evangelism* (Nashville, TN: Thomas Nelson, 2011), v.

[15] Jeremy Walker, *The Brokenhearted Evangelist* (Grand Rapids, MI: Reformation Heritage Books, 2012), 33.

one-to-one evangelistic activity to bring more people to faith in Christ than any service, program, or event we sponsor.[16]

The Importance of Prayer

Lastly, prayer must not be overlooked when it comes to evangelism. Every gospel seed that is cast must be prayed over. Every field that is plowed with preaching must be rained on with supplication. We must pray for souls in the prayer meetings. Pray for souls at the supper table. Pray for souls in the closet. Wrestle with God for souls as Jacob did in Genesis. Plead in the name of Christ for more souls to be saved. Plead with God to give the gift of faith to the lost. Preach and pray. Preach and pray. This is biblical evangelism. And yet, sadly, we all know how often the prayer meetings are neglected: "At a certain meeting of ministers and church officers, one after another doubted the value of prayer meetings; all confessed that they had a very small attendance, and several acknowledged without the slightest compunction that they had quite given them up."[17] How can we expect souls to be saved if we have no genuine passion to see it happen? If churches are sluggish in their evangelism, it goes without saying they are probably not praying for souls to be saved, either. We must preach and pray.

Interestingly, George W. Robertson makes the observation that "the Bible never commands or even describes believers praying for people to be converted; rather, they pray for 'more

---

[16] John MacArthur, *Ashamed of the Gospel* (Wheaton, IL: Crossway Books, 1993), 194.

[17] Charles H. Spurgeon, "Another Word Concerning the Down-Grade," *The Sword and the Trowel* (August 1887), 397-398.

laborers' (Matt. 9:37), 'open doors' (Col. 4:3), and 'boldness' (Acts 4:29). The implication seems to be that praying for someone's heart to change would give the impression that somehow the power to convert lies within the person."[18] This contradicts what has been said regarding prayer for souls to be saved, but even Robertson cannot be entirely consistent in this area. The last sentence of his booklet reads: "And out of confidence in the sovereign grace of God, the tearful witness must pray that the Spirit would bring in his harvest of souls redounding to the praise of God's glorious grace."[19] Will Metzger agrees in *Tell the Truth*: "We should have a great expectancy in our prayers. God is willing and able to save a great number of people."[20] Also J.I. Packer reminds us to "pray for those whom we seek to win, that the Holy Spirit will open their hearts; and we should pray for ourselves in our own witness."[21] John Owen agrees, saying about the lost, "Our duty is to pray that God would pour forth his Spirit even on them also, who will quickly cause them to 'look on him whom they have pierced, and mourn.'"[22]

Perhaps the reason some are hesitant to pray for souls to be saved, especially in a church context, is because increased numbers leads to increased problems and demands:

> Believers may fear that if they pray for more numbers in their local church, God will hear and actually answer them. Priorities then come into play, because if there are more people, there are going to be more problems with

---

[18] George W. Robertson, *What is Evangelism?* (Phillipsburg, NJ: P&R, 2013), 6.

[19] Robertson, *What is Evangelism?*, 48.

[20] Will Metzger, *Tell the Truth* (Downers Grove, IL: InterVarsity, 1981), 207.

[21] J.I. Packer, *Evangelism and the Sovereignty of God* (Downers Grove, IL: InterVarsity Press, 1961), 119-120.

[22] John Owen, *The Work of the Spirit* (Carlisle, PA: The Banner of Truth Trust: 1967), 315.

seating, room may be at a premium, and the church is probably going to have to spend more money. Therefore, some might think that common sense dictates that it is foolish to pray for increased numbers in the church.[23]

As nonsensical as this may seem, it is a genuine trial for churches whenever prayers for more people are answered. Wes Bredenhof provides the proper response to such an attitude when he says God "will provide the means," and that "we can pray fervently for God to grow our churches. We can pray that He add to our numbers, not for the sake of numbers but for the glory of His name and because we genuinely care about our unbelieving friends and neighbors."[24] Prayer for souls will also teach us to be more tender towards the lost, and praying for our evangelism efforts will teach us to take ownership of the seed that has been cast. It will help us to feel the distress which sinners ought to feel for their own souls. It will help us grieve that Christ has been held up to sinners, yet they have not believed. It will cause us to participate in the sufferings of Christ, which will in turn help us to love Him more.

Even if Robertson is not entirely consistent in his booklet, he does provide a great resource regarding how to pray when it comes to evangelism. First, more laborers are badly needed when it comes to evangelism, now as in the times of Christ. And just as importantly, we should pray that more pastors are raised up who are burdened for evangelism. No pastor would claim to have a dislike for evangelism, but we are known by our fruit. Very few Reformed pastors are actively engaged in evangelism.

---

[23] Bredenhof, *To Win Our Neighbors for Christ*, 57.
[24] Bredenhof, *To Win Our Neighbors for Christ*, 58.

This is not meant to be a cheap shot at pastors, but rather a call to pray for our church leaders. Their example is always important, and no less so when it comes to their approach to evangelism. Second and third, we must pray for boldness and open doors when we evangelize. It is one thing for a door of evangelism to be opened to us. It is another thing to approach that door boldly. The Holy Spirit is our only aid when it comes to bold evangelism, as well as providing situations to do so: "Thus, when believers have this gospel treasure in Christ, the comfort of belonging to Him, the Holy Spirit not only compels them to love their lost neighbors, but He also gives them the strength to share the gospel."[25]

The Die Is Cast

Some are called to exotic lands where conversions are taking place by the thousands. Some have lived in seasons when revival sweeps through villages like wildfire. Some, like most of us, have been called to evangelize in the iron-clad soil of the contemporary West. Where should we look for comfort? What can we grab hold of for hope?

First, the *Second London Baptist Confession* reminds us that where the gospel goes forth is the Lord's prerogative alone:

The particular nations and individuals who are granted this revelation are chosen solely according to the sovereign will and good pleasure of God. This choice does not depend on any promise to those who demonstrate good stewardship of their natural abilities based on common

---

[25] Bredenhof, *To Win Our Neighbors for Christ*, 55.

light received apart from the gospel. No one has ever done this nor can anyone do so. Therefore, in every age the preaching of the gospel to individuals and nations has been granted in widely varying degrees of expansion and contraction, according to the counsel of the will of God.[26]

Like those who have gone before us under similar circumstances, we must know "that times and seasons are ordered by God and...that every era of great advance has generally been preceded by the establishment of firm doctrinal foundations through years of patient sowing, accompanied not infrequently by suffering."[27] We must patiently sow the seeds of the gospel, regardless of the consequence or soil.

Second, even though these are by no means golden days for Christianity in the West, if God sends revival in our day, so be it. But if not, as Daniel's friends told Nebuchadnezzar (Dan. 3:18), let us resolve, regardless of the cost, to use only biblically prescribed methods of evangelism and to do it for the glory of God, not "the one." Faithfulness must be our goal, not numbers. Our comfort will be to know that God is pleased with our aim and our method. The most important thing to remember about evangelism is that we should do it because we love Christ. God gets a special kind of glory when we evangelize in the midst of apparent unfruitfulness. We prove to the world that He is worthy to proclaim, even when His work in the conversion of the lost is unapparent. We should be bold and outspoken in our evangelism, because Christ is worthy: "This is certainly no time for weak men, weak messages, and

---

[26] Ch. 20.3
[27] Murray, *The Puritan Hope*, 235.

weak ministries. What is needed is moral strength and courage and uncompromising proclamation of the truth that can set people free."[28]

R. B. Kuiper notes that "at times, even over extended periods, it may seem to him that the seed of the gospel sown by him has fallen only by the wayside or in stony places or among thorns, and that none of it has sprouted in good ground.... With God as his leader, he will never despair. His love for God...will keep him from falling into the slough of despondency."[29] When we evangelize because we love God, first and foremost, we will never be dissuaded whenever faced by various trials. When we evangelize for the sake of God's glory, not "the one," such "love for God and His Christ will induce, yes compel, God's child to devote himself wholeheartedly to the spread of the evangel."[30] Such a single-minded focus on God will keep us from shrinking back, regardless of our evangelism's outcome.

Onward, Christian Soldier!

Evangelism is one of the primary reasons we are left on earth. In the Old Testament, the Lord kept the Israelites in constant warfare so that they would not grow dull and lazy. The same could be said of us when it comes to the warfare of evangelism. We have a task to do on earth, especially as it relates to the lost souls around us. There is a reason why Jesus emphasized evangelism in His last words to the disciples: "It appears that he regarded evangelism as the very reason for their being...If

---

[28] John MacArthur, *Ashamed of the Gospel* (Wheaton, IL: Crossway Books, 1993), 46.

[29] R.B. Kuiper, *God-Centered Evangelism* (Carlisle, PA: The Banner of Truth, 1966), 103.

[30] Kuiper, *God-Centered Evangelism*, 105.

the disciples truly loved their Lord, they would carry out his call to evangelize. It was not an optional matter for them."[31]

This is why the Christian should never be bored or restless. So long as the lost are around, he has a mission to undertake. Whether or not "the one" is saved, the Lord is glorified whenever the mission is pursued. Warfare also keeps us sharp in other areas of our Christian life. Jeremy Walker rightly notices that "there is little that so elevates us—that so engages the totality of our redeemed humanity—as the holy cut and thrust of evangelism."[32] His description of evangelism as a means of grace reads like a passionate answer in a catechism:

> How do we keep our prayers fiery? By engaging in hand-to-hand combat with Satan's hosts, for those who are yet under his dominion. Why do we keep our spiritual weapons sharp? So that we can fight. How do we learn how to use those weapons? When we engage with lost men. Where are our graces brought to their highest pitch and exercised to their greatest degree? It is often when we are locked in mortal combat for the salvation of a soul.[33]

When it comes to evangelism, things are not getting easier. Eventually evangelism could be outlawed. Eventually Christians who evangelize in the West may be jailed. Or perhaps the Holy Spirit will be poured out in a fresh way on the West, and bold evangelism will become welcomed by the entire hemisphere. We don't know. But regardless of what happens, let us resolve to go forth into the vineyards of the Lord, sharing

---

[31] Millard Erickson, *Christian Theology*, (Grand Rapids, MI: Baker, 1983), 1061.

[32] Walker, *The Brokenhearted Evangelist*, 30.

[33] Walker, *The Brokenhearted Evangelist*, 29.

Christ with everyone we come into contact with, even if none are saved. Francis Schaeffer, who saw himself as an evangelist above all else, reminds us that evangelism will not always be successful, yet we still have a task to perform:

> Christianity is not a modern success story. It is to be preached with love and tears into the teeth of men, preached without compromise, without regard to the world's concept of success. If there seem to be no results, remember that Jeremiah did not see the results in his day. They came later. If there seem to be no results, it does not change God's imperative. It is simply up to you and to me to go on, go on, go on, whether we see the results or whether we don't. Go on.[34]

Although it seems very few people are being saved in the West, what must be avoided is using such a climate as an excuse for not expecting people to be saved each time we share the gospel. God's Word never returns void, whether or not a person is saved, but we must vigorously expect people to be converted whenever the gospel is communicated. We must have an ardent belief in God's power and desire to save souls. As Spurgeon says, we must "have great faith in the Word of God and in the power of the message to save people."[35] Even in a climate like ours, God still uses the foolishness of the cross to turn sinners to Him. When it comes to soul-winning, we must be of Rachel's demeanor, saying to the Lord, "give me children else I die!"[36]

---

[34] Francis A. Schaeffer, *Death in the City* (Wheaton, IL: Crossway, 1969), 94-95.

[35] Charles H. Spurgeon, *The Soul Winner* (Abbotsford, WI: Life Sentence Publishing, 2016), 45.

[36] Spurgeon, *The Soul Winner*, 37.

We must not be satisfied with little or no salvific fruit. On the contrary, we must aim for fruit. We must genuinely care whether or not people get saved. We must never be satisfied with our evangelism efforts if the people we evangelize are not converted. There is more work to be done. There are more fields to enter into. And yet, as John Calvin notes, "we are too apt to conclude that our attempts at reclaiming the ungodly are vain and ineffectual, and forget that God is able to crown them with success."[37] Far from celebrating the lack of genuine conversions in the contemporary West, may this book be an exhortation to keep the field no matter the outcome, and to remember that "the Lord God is in your midst, a mighty one who will save" (Zeph. 3:17).

---

[37] John Calvin, *Commentaries* (Grand Rapids: Baker, 1996), 5:302.

BIBLIOGRAPHY

Alexander, Archibald. *Practical Truths*. Harrisonburg, VA: Sprinkle Publications, 1998.

———. *Thoughts on Religious Experience*. 1844; reprint Carlisle, PA: The Banner of Truth Trust, 1967.

Augustine. *City of God*. Translated by Marcus Dods. New York: Random House, 1993.

Baker, Al. "Three Reasons We Need Evangelists." The Banner of Truth Trust, 2017.

———. "What the Civil Magistrate Can and Cannot Do." *Forget None of His Benefits Newsletter*, Vol. 17, Number 44 (Nov 8, 2018).

Bahnsen, Greg. *Van Til's Apologetic*. Phillipsburg, N.J.: P&R Publishing, 1998.

Bayly, Timothy B. "Foreword" to *Persecution in the Early Church*. Bloomington, IL: Clearnote Press, 2014.

Berkhof, Louis. *Systematic Theology*. Carlisle, PA: The Banner of Truth, 1958.

Boston, Thomas. *The Art of Man-Fishing*. Ross-shire, Scotland: Christian Focus Publications, 1998.

Bredenhof, Wes. *To Win Our Neighbors for Christ*. Grand Rapids, MI: Reformation Heritage Books, 2015.

Busenitz, Nathan. "The Word of Truth in a World of Error." *Evangelism*. Nashville, TN: Thomas Nelson, 2011.

Calvin, John. Tr. John Pringle. *Commentary on the Epistles of Paul the Apostle to the Corinthians*, 2015.

———. *Institutes of the Christian Religion*. Edited by John McNeill. Louisville, Ky.: Westminster Press, 1960.

Carey, William (Letter to Mary Carey and Ann Hobson, December 22, 1796). *The Journal and Selected Letters of William Carey*. Edited by Terry G. Carter. Macon, GA: Smyth & Helwys, 2000.

Chantry, Walter J. *Today's Gospel*. Carlisle, PA: The Banner of Truth, 1970.

Charnock, Stephen. *The Existence and Attributes of God*. 1853; reprint Grand Rapids, MI: Baker Books, 2005.

Chesterman, A. de M. "The Journals of Daniel Brainerd and of William Carey." *The Baptist Quarterly* 19 (1961-62).

Clark, Gordon H. *Today's Evangelism: Counterfeit or Genuine?* Unicoi, TN: The Trinity Foundation, 1990.

Damer, T. Edward. *Attacking Faulty Reasoning.* Belmont, CA: Wadsworth, 2001.

Denton, Ryan and Scott Smith. *A Certain Sound: A Primer on Open Air Preaching.* Grand Rapids, MI: Reformation Heritage Books, 2019.

Dever, Mark. *Nine Marks of a Healthy Church.* Wheaton, IL: Crossway, 2000.

Erickson, Millard. *Christian Theology.* Grand Rapids, MI: Baker, 1983.

Evans, William. *Open Air Preaching.* New York, NY: Fleming H. Revell Company, 1901.

Forrester, Duncan B. "Martin Luther and John Calvin." *History of Political Philosophy.* Edited by Leo Strauss and Joseph Cropsey. Chicago: University of Chicago Press, 1963.

Green, Michael. *Evangelism in the Early Church.* Grand Rapids, MI: Wm. B Eerdmans Publishing Company, 1970.

Gurnall, William. *The Christian in Complete Armour.* 1662; reprint London: The Banner of Truth, 1964.

Haykin, Michael H. G. *The Missionary Fellowship of William Carey.* Sanford, FL: Reformation Trust Publishing, 2018.

Jones, John Morgan and William Morgan. *The Calvinistic Methodist Fathers of Wales*, Vol. 1. Carlisle, PA: The Banner of Truth Trust, 1890.

Kohler, Joe. *The Forgotten Officer.* Bloomington, IN: WestBow Press, 2016.

Kuiper, R.B. *God-Centered Evangelism.* Carlisle, PA: The Banner of Truth, 1966.

Latourette, Kenneth. *A History of the Expansion of Christianity.* New York: Harper, 1944.

Lawson, Stephen J. "Introduction" to *The Missionary Fellowship of William Carey.* Sanford, FL: Reformation Trust Publishing, 2018.

LifeSiteNews. "Switzerland votes overwhelmingly to jail citizens for 'homophobia,' 'transphobia.'" Accessed February 21, 2019. https://www.lifesitenews.com/news/switzerland-votes-overwhelmingly-to-jail-citizens-for-homophobia-transphobi.

Lloyd-Jones, D. Martyn. *Studies in the Sermon on the Mount.* Grand Rapids: WM. B. Eerdman's, 1984.

———. *The Presentation of the Gospel.* London: Inter-Varsity Fellowship, 1949.

MacArthur, John. *Ashamed of the Gospel.* Wheaton, IL: Crossway Books, 1993.

———. "Theology of Sleep," *Evangelism.* Nashville, TN: Thomas Nelson, 2011.

———. *Strange Fire.* Nashville, TN: Nelson Books, 2013.

MacArthur, John and Jesse Johnson. "Rediscovering Biblical Evangelism." *Evangelism.* Nashville, TN: Thomas Nelson, 2011.

MacMullen, Ramsay. *Christianizing the Roman Empire.* Yale University, 1984.

Donald A. McGavron, *Understanding Church Growth.* Grand Rapids, MI: Wm. B. Eerdmans, 1970.

Metzger, Will. *Tell the Truth.* Downers Grove, IL: InterVarsity, 1981.

Morgan, J. Vyrnwy. *The Welsh Religious Revival*, 1904-5: A Retrospect and a Criticism. London, 1909.

Murray, Iain H. *Revival and Revivalism*. Carlisle, PA: The Banner of Truth Trust, 1994.

———. *The Puritan Hope*. Carlisle, PA: The Banner of Truth, 1971.

North American Mission Board (SBC). Accessed August 10, 2018. www.namb.net/go.

Owen, John. *The Work of the Spirit*. Carlisle, PA: The Banner of Truth Trust, 1967.

Reisinger, Ernest C. *Today's Evangelism*. Philipsburg, NJ: Craig Press, 1982.

Robertson, George W. *What is Evangelism?* Phillipsburg, NJ: P&R, 2013.

Rushdoony, Rousas John. *By What Standard*. Vallecito, CA: Ross House, 1995.

Salter, Darius. *American Evangelism*. Grand Rapids, MI: Baker Book House, 1996.

Schaeffer, Francis A. *Death in the City*. Wheaton, IL: Crossway, 1969.

Smith, George. *The Life of William Carey*. Edinburgh: R&R Clark, 1885.

Sproul, R. C. *The Consequences of Ideas: Understanding the Concepts That Shaped Our World*. Wheaton, Ill.: Crossway, 2000.

———. *Essential Truths of the Christian Faith*. Carol Stream, Ill.: Tyndale House, 1992.

Spurgeon, Charles H. *An All-Round Ministry*. Carlisle, PA: Banner of Truth, repr. 1965.

———. "Another Word Concerning the Down-Grade." *The Sword and the Trowel*, August 1887.

———. "Holding Fast the Faith." The Metropolitan Tabernacle Pulpit, Vol. 34. London: Passmore and Alabaster, 1888.

———. *Lectures to My Students*. Grand Rapids: Zondervan, 1980.

———. "Soul Saving Our One Business." *The Metropolitan Tabernacle Pulpit*, Vol. 25. London: Passmore & Alabaster, 1879.

———. *The Soul Winner*. Abbotsford, WI: Life Sentence Publishing, 2016.

———. "The Great Sin of Doing Nothing," Christian Classics Ethereal Library, 1886, Vol. 32, No. 1916, 1886, https://www.ccel.org/ccel/spurgeon/sermons32.xl.html. Accessed February 20, 2019.

Smith, Morton H. *Reformed Evangelism*. Clinton, MS: Multi-Communication Ministries, 1975.

Sproul, R. C. *Essential Truths of the Christian Faith*. Carol Stream, IL: Tyndale House Publishers, 1992.

Stott, John. *Christian Mission in the Modern World*. Downers Grove, IL: Intervarsity Press, 1975.

Terry, John Mark. *Evangelism: A Concise History*. New York, NY: Broadman & Holman, 1994.

Tertullian. "Apology." *The Ante-Nicene Fathers*. Edited by Alexander Roberts and James Donaldson. Peabody, MA: Hendrickson, 1994.

The Wee Flea. "The Hate Police Are Now Here." Accessed February 21, 2019. https://theweeflea.com/2018/10/02/the-hate-police-are-now-here/.

Tertullian. "On Idolatry." *The Ante-Nicene Fathers*. Edited by Alexander Roberts and James Donaldson. Peabody, MA: Hendrickson, 1994.

Van Til, Cornelius. *Christianity in Conflict*. Philadelphia: Westminster Theological Seminary, 1962–1964 (syllabus).

———. *An Introduction to Systematic Theology*. Nutley, N.J.: Presbyterian and Reformed, 1974.

———. *The Reformed Pastor and Modern Thought*. Nutley, N.J.: Presbyterian and Reformed, 1971.

Wagner, C. Peter. *Church Growth and the Whole Gospel*. San Francisco: Harper & Row, 1981.

Walker, Jeremy. *The Brokenhearted Evangelist*. Grand Rapids, MI: Reformation Heritage Books, 2012.

Wholesome Words Home. "The Serampore Form of Agreement (1805)." Accessed February 21, 2019. www.wholesomewords.org/missions/bcarey13.html.

Workman, Herbert. *Persecution in the Early Church*. Bloomington, IL: Clearnote Press, 2014.